Routes of Berlandier's
Travels in Texas in 1828
Based upon Stephen F. Austin's Map of 1829
And that of the U.S. National Museum

BERLANDIER

A French Naturalist
On The Texas Frontier

A Novel by
James Kaye

Order this book online at www.trafford.com
or email orders@trafford.com

Most Trafford titles are also available at major online book retailers.

The views expressed in this work are solely those of the author and do not necessarily reflect the
views of the publisher, and the publisher hereby disclaims any responsibility for them.

Printed in the United States of America.

ISBN: 978-1-4269-4053-8 (sc)
ISBN: 978-1-4269-8496-9 (e)

Trafford rev. 04/21/2012

www.trafford.com

North America & international
toll-free: 1 888 232 4444 (USA & Canada)
phone: 250 383 6864 ♦ fax: 812 355 4082

CONTENTS

For
Anyone interested in the
Frontier history Of Texas
And that of the French naturalist
Jean Louis (Jon-Louie) Berlandier
(1805-1851)

PREFACE

After publication in Europe in 1826 of botanist Jean Louis (Jon-Louie) Berlandier's scholarly work on gooseberries, *Memoire sur la famille des Grossulariees,* his expertise in plant morphology and taxonomy came to the attention of a group from the Academy of Natural Sciences in Geneva, Switzerland, in need of a naturalist to collect plant and animal specimens for them in Mexico. Included in the prestigious group was Berlandier's botany professor, Dr. Augustin Pyramus De Candolle who highly recommended his promising young student for the position and in the effort, if so willing, Berlandier would follow in the steps of naturalists José Mociño, Martin de Sessé, Pablo de la Llave, and the illustrious German naturalist Baron Alexander von Humboldt who was a favorite of Berlandier's to read of one's works.

Each had given already much attention to the flora and fauna of the, then, "New Spain" under Spanish rule, but following the Mexican revolution of 1810-1821 New Spain was known by Berlandier's time as the "Republic of Mexico." However, little attention by either Spain or Mexico had been given to the flora and fauna of the northernmost State of *Coahuila y Tejas*, and much of Berlandier's work in that region of the new world became devoted also to the ethnology of the indigenous Indians in Texas and of their uses of native plants for foods and pharmaceutical purposes.

It was after a knock on the office door of Professor De Candolle in Geneva that the following story begins, based largely on the voluminous journal of Berlandier's odyssey [*Voyage au Mexique par Louis Berlandier pendant les années 1826 à 1834*] but also on the diaries and other writings of Berlandier's contemporaries, General Manuel de Mier y Terán, Joseph Chambers Clopper, Rafael Chowel (also spelled Chovel), Juan Antonio Padilla, José María Sánchez y Tapia, José Francisco Ruiz, and the scholarly works of De Candolle himself.

Other references for this novel are those of Colonel Richard Irving Dodge of the U.S. Army who fought numerous of the Plains Indian tribes in Texas and elsewhere; of the more than thirty tribes of Indians in Texas specifically studied by Jean Louis Berlandier; of ethnologists

William Bollaert, W. W. Newcomb, and John C. Ewers who wrote of them; and of artist George Catlin who painted, so he believed, "some of the wildest tribes in North America" including especially the Comanche (**Fig. 4**, p. 85) in Texas known in literature as the "Terrors of the Plains" synonymous with "wildness, fierceness and treachery."

Other, numerous, references of importance are also listed in the Bibliography at the end of this novel along with Appendix "A" listing some sixty different plant and animal species named after Berlandier in honor of his contributions to natural science. Also included are pictures (**Plates 1-5**) of a few of the better known plants and animals collected by him.

He is however best known for his treatise of *The Indians of Texas in 1830,* first written in French then translated into English with an introduction by American historian/ethnologist John C. Ewers who believed that the author was "one of the most enlightened amateur ethnographers of the American West during the frontier period." But how could Berlandier have known nearly two centuries ago that he would, today, be considered as one of the most accomplished writers of New World aborigines. Or, how could Berlandier have known when leaving his homeland in 1826 that he would spend the rest of his life on the Texas frontier, never to return. And what a change it must have been for him to leave the towering snow-covered French and Swiss Alps to the flatland heat and aridity of southern Texas and northeastern Mexico. Moreover, what a change it must have been for Berlandier to leave the wealth and intellect of Europe to the poverty and illiteracy of the Latin America of his time.

Much of what is known of Berlandier from the time of his birth until his untimely death in 1851 at little more than 46 years of age comes primarily from his diaries and journals, and from those of his contemporaries who traveled with him. There are historical accounts of his participation in the Mexican-American War of 1846-1848 when he was a Captain *Aide-de-camp* interpreter to Mexican General Mariano Arista, as well as being a cartographer of the Palo Alto Battlefield near Brownsville.

There is an additional wealth of Berlandier's many letters, manuscripts and drawings in Institutions as the Smithsonian, Library of Congress, United States National Museum and libraries at Harvard and Yale, There are notes and collections of his plants in twenty-seven world herbaria; and notes of geological, celestial, meteorological, and other observations in many libraries including records of his travels in the Center For American History at The University of Texas, Austin, and one of the finest collections of Comanche regalia and artifacts made by Berlandier is on display in the Gilchrest Museum in Tulsa, Oklahoma.

Following his participation as a biologist and anthropologist for the 1827-1829 Mexican Boundary Commission surveys, Berlandier lived the remainder of his professional life in Matamoros, Tamaulipas. There, too, Berlandier became a pharmacist, doctor, and a participant in a pharmaceutical business; an administrator for the Matamoros hospitals during the Mexican American War; and always an avid collector of plants and animals in various parts of Texas and Mexico; several were new to science and many others discovered by other botanists through many years were named in his honor (Appendix "A").

Beyond all of that, however, little is known of Berlandier's personal life. Little is known of his French family or even with certainty the date of his birth though believed to have been about 1805 in Fort de l'Écluse, France, near its border with Switzerland and close to Geneva where he studied pharmacy, and botany at the Academy of Natural Sciences. Moreover, little is known of his Mexican wife or even her name, or of a reported several children and, it can be assumed of still living descendents. But who of them to what other names, and where now located, and to what other accomplishments remain unknown except that a son is said to have been a Lieutenant of Artillery in the Mexican Army.

Much of the "unknowns" of Berlandier's life can only be imagined or assumed to have happened but mixed with what *is* known about him and presented herein in the form of a historical novel; the freedoms and benefits of creative writing. And that privilege in this case is *Berlandier; A French Naturalist on the Texas Frontier*. All characters are persons true to history but for purposes of the narration some chronological facts are altered. All dialogue is duly fictionalized though befitting to the subjects, topics, and events of the times in Berlandier's 1820s era on the Texas Frontier.

The following story takes place in the period between the years of 1826 and 1828 when Jean Louis Berlandier first signed on as a biologist member of the Boundary Commission of the Mexican Ministry of the Interior to explore the vast, then, wildernesses of Texas north of Laredo on the Rio Grande River or *Rio Bravo del Norte* north and east of San Antonio known then as San Antonio de Béxar or, simply, only as Béxar.

The odyssey begins in Geneva, Switzerland, on a day late in 1826 with a knock on a door for an interview.

James Kaye

BERLANDIER

Chapter One

THE INTERVIEW
Geneva, 1826

"Please enter, and please sit" Professor Augustin De Candolle asked in French as he motioned Louis (Louie) Berlandier to a chair next to his cluttered roll-top desk with pigeonholes crammed. Atop along with a plume pen and ink well lay handwritten pages of the professor's manuscript *Prodromus Systematis Naturalis Regni Vegetablis* long already in his writing of a flora of the world. Across tops of adjacent dusty tables lay scattered herbarium sheets, and under the tables sat stacks of plant presses tightly packed with botanical specimens drying between sheets of old newspapers. Along one wall there stood ceiling-high book cases and along other walls herbarium cases stacked two deep and when opened the materials within scented the room with the un-mistakable aroma of naphthalene crystals used as repellents for insect pests.

"What is this plant?" De Candolle asked as he handed a pressed specimen to Berlandier curious as to why he had just been asked such a question, or even to be there; but surely not to identify a plant. Berlandier couldn't imagine, as De Candolle was considered to be the most renowned of the world's botanists of his time.

"Surely you don't need *me* to identify this for you," Berlandier remarked facetiously with a wry grin.

"Oh no!" the professor smiled in reply. "I already know the plant, but I want to know if **you** know it, at least as to its family."

Berlandier studied the plant for a moment and replied that it was obviously a composite of some kind with the characteristic ray and disc flowers and the involucral bracts characteristic of the Astraea [sunflowers]. "The stigmatic lines suggest that it's some variety of an aster," he answered, "but it's not one I'm familiar with here in Europe."

"Very good!" De Candolle replied with a smile. "It is *not* from Europe. But what about this one?" the professor asked as he handed Berlandier still another pressed and dried specimen.

"Well…it's clearly a thistle of some sort with the spiny leaf margins and the nature of the involucral bracts. There are no ray flowers…only disc flowers typical of thistles in the Cynareae."

"You're correct again," De Candolle replied. "It *is* a thistle of the Cynareae, but also not from Europe."

"What about this one?" De Candolle asked as he handed Berlandier another pressed specimen.

With little hesitation Berlandier identified it as a mint of some sort identifiable by the typical characteristic square stems and opposite leaves. "The flowers whorled in the upper leaf axils are a bit puzzling though," Berlandier remarked, casually. "The mints that I know have flowers at the tips of stems on short stalks, not quite like these."

"Well, it *is* a mint…but what about this one?" De Candolle asked as he handed Berlandier yet another pressed specimen.

"I'm not sure with this one. It's a bit more of a puzzle," Berlandier replied as he studied the plant for a long moment. "It's mint-like…like something in the Lamiales…but the ovary isn't lobed typical of mints. Moreover, the stem isn't as square as mints should be…but I would guess it's closely allied."

"Very good!" De Candolle replied again with a smile. "It's one of the verbenas that occur principally in the Western Hemisphere but not here in Europe. Verbenas and mints as you know are in the same Order, so you *are* correct to determine the two are closely related.

"What about this plant?" De Candolle asked to further test Berlandier's botanical expertise. De Candolle needed to know with some certainty just how expertise his student was in plant morphology and taxonomy.

"It's not quite like anything I've ever seen," he replied. "The claw-like spines are similar to those in the Rosales…and the seed pods obviously suggest a legume of some kind. The curlicue shapes are most interesting however. Strange!" he remarked. "I've never seen a bean pod shaped like this one."

"Well you're correct again on that. It *is* a legume…a bean…but not a species you would know. It is one of the so-called cat-claw acacias from the desert southwest of the New World. As a matter of fact, this one and the others that I've just shown you all came from Mexico sent here to the Academy from the collections of Mociño, Sessé, and De la Llave though much of the Sessé material is down in Madrid. He was kind enough however to send some here for my work on the flora of the world and the first that any of us here had seen."

"I envy anyone's opportunities to have collected plants in Mexico," Berlandier remarked, "as I've read of Alexander von Humboldt's expeditions in Mexico and South America…'Old Spain' he wrote of the area."

"That leads into why I wanted you here today. The Academy is impressed with your monograph on the European Grossularieae and research into flower and seed reproduction of Bellflowers. In fact, I am citing and excerpting parts of your works for my *Prodromus*."

"Well, I must say that I'm honored." Berlandier responded with a big grin and with a feeling of no little amount of pride in recognition of his work and expertise.

"Moreover," De Candolle continued, "I have a letter from a former student of mine now in Mexico, a Señor Lucas Alamán, who is now the Minister of Foreign Affairs for the newly established republic. He wants my recommendations on the appointment of a biologist to accompany an expedition of the Comisión de Limites [Border Commission] being organized to explore the northernmost province of Coahuila y Téjas, that part north of the Rio Bravo. An earlier Report by Juan Antonio Padilla, a former cavalry officer stationed in San Antonio de Béxar, has contributed much knowledge already on the natives of that little explored region but the Ministry wants additional information, especially on the plants and animals of the region. I am recommending you for the post if…as you say…you are envious of biologists who've already collected in Mexico. Are you willing? And if so, the position will offer you opportunities if you want to investigate the New World gooseberries and bellflowers, and anything else to your interest of the botany."

"I would be delighted for the chance…and honor it…but as you well know I am trained more as a pharmacist in the medicinal uses of plants than as a botanist."

"That's all the better and more of what's wanted. It's obvious your knowledge of plant morphology and taxonomy is equivalent to the best of my students as you've just demonstrated by your identifications. And pharmacy trained as well as a botanist you will be helpful to the Ministry to know the uses of native plants by the indigenes. Moreover, you are quite obviously an astute observer and prolific writer. Your systematic treatment of the Grossularieae and that of reproduction in the Campanulaceae attests to it or I wouldn't have cited your previous work, or now recommend you for the expedition in Mexico and Texas."

"Well, as I say, I will be honored...and the opportunity to investigate new kinds of plants intrigues me."

"I understand from Alamán that José María Sánchez y Tapia will accompany your group to write of the expedition's travels, but both of you need to be forewarned. It was with good reason that the Spanish in that part of the world have said that Mexico and its Texas province are "inhabited by barbarians and wild beasts" and the aborigines thought of as *barbárico*. 'Barbarous' is what Padilla wrote of them. The Dutch trappers early in America thought of the indigenous Indians as *barbaars*. The French Black Robes who like the Spanish Brown Robes, and who tried to convert Indians to Christianity and largely failed, spoke of them as *Les Sauvages*...certainly true enough from the nature of their unholy barbarism. The lives and moralities of primitive aborigines in the new world as you will find, are nothing akin or even close to what Christian peoples elsewhere in the world teach and believe of 'love thy neighbor.'

"The few villages in Texas are widely scattered, and for good reason are clustered mostly around military posts, or *presidios* as they are called in Mexico, for protection. As well known in that part of the world it is not safe to travel in areas of the natives except in well armed groups, and Alamán assures me for safety in the field that the expedition will be escorted by well-armed mounted troops. You, too, will be supplied with a horse, rifle, pistol and other necessities by Alamán and the military, and your expenses will be reimbursed by the Ministry. Before you leave I will supply you with a microscope, telescope, hygrometer, barometer, thermometer, compass, needed reference books, and all of the presses and other herbarium materials you will need for collecting plants including jars and formalin for preserving animal specimens. We will pay you a certain amount in francs commensurate with the numbers of specimens that you collect and ship here. Are you interested?"

"Of *course* I am, and when can I leave? As you know," the eager and now excited Berlandier hastened to add in support of his enthusiasm and availability, "I am not married, so an early date to leave is of no problem with me."

"Then plan for a passage on the American made schooner *Hannah Elizabeth* scheduled to depart Le Havre-de-Grâce for Tampico de Tamaulipas on October 14 [1826] in order to have no danger at that time of the year of summertime hurricanes. The long voyage will take at least two months and I will make arrangements with Mr. Charles Roding, the Captain, who informs me that there will be a small number of other passengers as travel companions and, he hopes," Professor De Candolle chuckled, "that none of you will get seasick."

So it was that Jean Louis (Jon-Louie, or simply Louie) Berlandier at little more than twenty years of age left Geneva for Mexico and probably with no thought that he would spend the rest of his life in the country of his destination and never to return.

Chapter Two
VOYAGE OF THE *HANNAH ELIZABETH*

Jean Louis Berlandier remained for a few days in Geneva studying through Baron von Humboldt's works on the plants and animals of the "New World;" the extensive herbarium housed in the Academy of Sciences in Geneva maintained by De Candolle; visited his family and friends to bid all farewell; and then as planned sailed out of Le Havre de Grâce on October 14, 1826, aboard the gaff-rigged top-sailed American schooner the *Hannah Elizabeth* (**Fig. 1** painting by Georgina Nemethy entitled *Schooner at Sea.*)

Leaving on an ebbing tide and a favorable wind the schooner under a full set of her canvas mains, staysails, jibs, and the towering topsails soon carried the crew and several passengers out into the wind-swept English Channel.

Soon thereafter it happened as it often does that some of the passengers inclined to it became seasick and when further out into the Trades with stronger winds and bigger seas the matter grew worse for some aboard that lasted the first few days. Fortunately, Berlandier was not so affected the entire voyage, not even that the *Hannah Elizabeth* sailed well-heeled at times awash with spray and rolling in never-ending swells. Berlandier wrote in his diary that he "could not complain in any manner about his voyage."

What he liked most in the quiet times of his bunk was to listen to the creaks and moaning groans of a wooden vessel and to hear the occasional slaps of sails or sounds of waves cresting against the hull and washing-down the decks. On most mornings before the dawn Berlandier was up on deck to enjoy the sunrises which he thought were some of the loveliest sights that Nature bestows; and especially the brightening colors of the sky and clouds as each sun arose.

Moreover, the avid naturalist took delight in observing and making detailed notes of the many animals including sea birds, dolphins and fish seen along the way starting when leaving port and seeing great numbers of jellyfish floating in the water. "Their numbers, sizeable at first," the observant naturalist wrote in his journal, "diminished so much that when we gained the high seas barely three or four leagues [one league equaling about three miles] from the coast we no longer saw them."

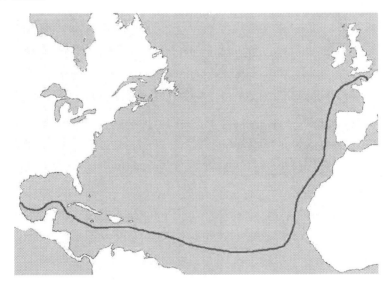

When finally clear of the Channel, the *Hannah Elizabeth* turned southerly (**Fig. 2**) under a full set of her canvas that drove the vessel hard at hull speed along the Southern Sailing Route west of the Azores off Spain and east of the Canaries off Morocco. Some of the land and shorebirds seen along the way suggested the proximity of land and, as Berlandier noted, "A raven, a sinister emblem of bad luck, came to rest on the mainmast as if to bid us a last farewell from Europe."

The *Hannah Elizabeth* continued on through the bluest of sapphire-colored seas; endless long-rolling cresting swells and waves with white caps; and with the whitest of fair weather clouds, those with flat bottoms and billowing tops. Such clouds were characteristic predictions of continuing good weather and seas, and the steady Trades that the Captain and crew always hoped for when circling the Southern Atlantic.

In its course (**Fig. 2**) the *Hannah Elizabeth* first sailed southward with the Portuguese and Canaries Currents, and then westward with the Caribbean flow to the Greater Antilles. The Trades remained good and by about mid-November, the schooner's crew and passengers began catching glimpses of more and more petrels, shearwaters, and frigate birds, and then more gannets and seagulls suggesting a nearing to yet unseen land.

Along the way Berlandier wrote of rafts of Sargassum weed in the Sargasso Sea that covered the area and that teemed with many species of "small marine animals such as barnacles." Strangely curious were tiny seahorses that looked to be the weed itself. But not so strange in that part of the southern Atlantic, to sailors, is that the Sargasso Sea is sometimes faint of wind and at times the *Hannah Elizabeth* just "ghosted along" with not even the faintest of a wake and when the sails flapped loosely.

But one afternoon when the wind was up, the passengers and crew spotted dolphins a short distance away. "They emerged from the waves at intervals," Berlandier wrote of them. "Their course was the same as ours and the sailors lost no time in predicting a change in the wind which in fact sprung up during the night. From long experiences of the 'ways of the seas,' sailors observed that porpoises and flying fish seemingly know to travel in the direction to a new wind which will prevail in a few hours. Thus," Berlandier wrote: "These animals can often guess the direction though how they know is unknown."

By means of his sextant, and by daily shootings of Polaris by night and the overhead noonday sun, the navigator plotted a course southward to latitude 18°N then eastward to the Caribbean. The helmsmen on two-hour shifts at the wheel followed the cockpit compass swinging back and forth on its gimbles in the rolling seas and with the needle-nosed bowsprit unerringly pointing the way.

Then it happened early one morning with eager anticipation since the day before when more and more seagulls were seen that all aboard came up on deck when hearing a shout of "Land Ho" from a crewman up in the crow's nest atop the mainmast. All caught a welcomed sight of the distant Lesser Antilles, the first land to be seen in more than a month after leaving the Canaries. In the course of another day under a full set of canvas the *Hannah Elizabeth* left the Atlantic and sailed into the eastern reaches of the Caribbean to the south of the Virgin Islands, steering clear of St. John to the north and St. Croix to the south and ever watchful in between for coral reefs.

For another few days of sometimes cloudy and at times squally weather, the schooner under variable winds and sail changes, and with following seas in the Caribbean Current, skirted the southerly picturesque shores of the Greater Antilles, first Puerto Rico, Haiti and the Dominican Republic and then Jamaica, "clearly seeing numerous villages and sugarcane plantations" that Berlandier noted in his journal. Of additional interest he wrote:

["After about the eighteenth degree of latitude we saw flying fish (*Exococtus volitans*) around the islands that leaped together by the hundreds from the water, sometimes landing on our deck. They arose a little above the surface of the waves and kept themselves in flight for quite a long time.

"The fish are incessantly pursued by many predators and scarcely do they leap out of the water than they are harassed by a host of seabirds swooping down on them from the air or flying close to the surface of the water to pursue the school. A species of gannet known in the Spanish islands as a booby is a relentless hunter of the flying fish. The boobies devour a great number of them, and in the waters of the Antilles the flying fish are practically its only food. Scarcely has the booby seized its prey, however, when frigate birds pursue and harass it until it lets go of the fish.

"Frequently the booby gets no more than the trouble of fishing, and the frigates that of pursuing and eating." (Paraphrased from Berlandier's Diary, Vol. 1, Chap. 1)]

With booms winged out and sails set wide for a downwind course, the *Hannah Elizabeth* sailed on ever westward and southward of Jamaica and to stay clear of the Caymans. The schooner then turned northward into the rougher Yucatan Channel with stronger winds and higher seas made more so with the additional speed of the now stronger Caribbean Current that transported immense amounts of water through the narrowed channel along with accompanying winds and cresting waves.

The Captain stayed mid-center of the Channel to avoid countercurrents in-close to Cuba and/or to Yucatan, and once clear of the peninsula the schooner sailed out into the quieter and more peaceful Bay of Campeche with its variable seas and breezes on a westerly course across to Mexico. And so it was on December 15, 1826, after two long months at sea that, at last, the *Hannah Elizabeth* lowered her sails and dropped anchor in the peaceful port of Santa Anna de Tampico a league inland of the mouth of the Río Pánuco. There too at anchor lay other vessels of her kind from a number of American ports and those from England, Germany, Cuba, the Antilles, and "fellow ships" from France.

["Thus we spent the first night at anchor, the very worst in our long crossing, and being anchored near to land and swamps, the mosquitoes, sand flies, and other pests did not allow us to sleep. The dew was so heavy by sunrise that it seemed to have rained in the night." (Paraphrased from Berlandier diary Vol. I Chapter 1)]

Notes: Information throughout this book set aside in brackets as that above is taken primarily from four different journals; Berlandier's *Journey To Mexico During The Years 1826 to 1834*, translated from French by Sheila M. Ohlendorf, Josette M. Bigelow, and Mary M. Standifer published by the Texas State Historical Association; *Texas by*

Terán edited by Jack Jackson, translated by John Wheat, and published by The University of Texas Press; *A Trip To Texas* by José María Sánchez, The Southwestern Historical Quarterly, Vol. XXIX, No. 4, April, 1936; and *Report On The Barbarous Indians Of The Province of Texas* by Juan Antonio Padilla, from the Austin Papers, University of Texas, Austin, translated by Mattie Austin Hatcher.

Moreover, information within brackets is quoted verbatim or is paraphrased and so stated, and such asides are said of by J. Frank Dobie (in Jenkins) as being "little touches of reality as necessary in historical narration as are salt and pepper to a soup or vegetable."

Furthermore, parenthesized information within brackets or elsewhere in the text are citations of other references listed in the Bibliography, and/or are the comments or hypotheses reflecting this author's own points of view that should not be charged to authors and/or to editors quoted from other works.

Chapter Three
THE MINISTRY OF FOREIGN AFFAIRS

Berlandier spent the next three months in Tampico exploring the environs and finding the town to be a small maritime *villa* situated on the left bank of the Rio Pánuco about five miles from the estuary and being little more than a "jumble of huts" as he wrote of them "belonging mostly to the coastal fishermen." When exploring the rivers, bays, swamps, bayous, and estuaries, Berlandier traveled by the only practical means, that of "long pirogues two to three feet wide and up to twenty or more feet long, hewn from the single trunks of cedar trees, and sometimes rigged with lateen sails" but complained of because of having round bottoms with no keels, and lacks of stability that make them easy to roll and difficult to row.

Of the plants, animals, and habitats in the region, Berlandier wrote of the principle agricultural crops being bananas and corn; but also pasturelands for cattle, and forest lands for wood products including growths of towering coconut palms. Of the several quadrupeds, Berlandier observed monkeys, deer, jaguars, cougars, peccaries, coatis, raccoons, wolves, coyotes, and the many hares and rabbits. Of the birds, the naturalist wrote of the "wading family" and of ducks, flamingos, and pelicans, and described roseate spoonbills as being "one of the most beautiful of birds in the New World."

He noted that "violent winds from the main will blow the soaring magnificent frigate birds inland," and of "charming hummingbirds flitting roundabout." Berlandier wrote of numerous caimans (*lagartos*) sunning on river banks and "everywhere flinging themselves into the water upon sighting approaching pirogues." (Paraphrased from Berlandier diary Vol. I: Chapter 2.)

After a sojourn of four months on the Gulf of Mexico during the winter and early months of spring "with the hot pestilential season rapidly approaching," Berlandier and his entourage departed on the third day of May, 1827, for the higher, cooler, interiors where foreigners preferred to live and who are not so much exposed to the dreaded yellow fever of warmer lowland areas.

> ["Señor Alamán who directed my travels advised me to go to Mexico City via the Huasteca, a well-known region in Mexico where the road is quite wide. Once along the way we stopped on a small prairie to collect plant specimens and where we were quite surprised to see a deer near to us." (Paraphrased from Berlandier Diary Vol. 1; Chapter 4)]

The route with the assistance of native Huastecan muleteers following the Rio Pánuco, Berlandier and his traveling party continued ever south-southwest to "Tantoyuca, entering hills which gradually rose higher and higher and where the vegetation became quite different from that of the preceding days." By the thirteenth of May, Berlandier reached the large village of Zacualtipán, arriving during a fiesta with music, dancing, and a bullfight never seen by him.

On the twentieth of May the odyssey continued with other stops along the way for rest, studies, and plant collections, reached Real del Monte. On the twenty-sixth day of May, Berlandier departed for his final destination of Mexico City that on arrival commented to it being "justly ranked among the most beautiful cities in the New World."

Soon thereafter and on formal presentation of himself at the Ministry of Foreign Affairs in the *Palacio Nacional*, Berlandier met the Minister, Sr. Lucas Alamán y Escalada, who had made the arrangements to appoint Berlandier as a biologist for the *Comisión de Límites* [Boundary Commission]. When furthering his own education in Europe, Alamán too had been a botany student of Professor A. P. De Candolle in Geneva thus explaining the relationships and Berlandier's appointment.

Alamán was born into a wealthy Spanish family in what then was New Spain in Guanajuato, Mexico, a gold and silver mining area, and who had studied geology and mining at the Royal School of Mines in Mexico City. There, he excelled in the fields of mineralogy, physics, chemistry and botany, and as a botanist grew and studied orchids.

In his honor, *Alamania* was a name given to a genus of orchids endemic to Mexico. As a historian, Alamán wrote a "History of Mexico" and was well received in giving a series of several *Lectures on the history of Mexico since the times of the Conquest by Spaniards in the late fifteenth century.*

With the formalities of their meeting over, and with his interests in Spaniard/Mesoamerican history, Alemán asked as a topic of conversation—but more as an inquiry into Berlandier's scopes of interest and abilities—"So, did you have any opportunities in Tampico and during your travels here to observe any of the plants and animals, and any of the indigenous peoples?"

"As a matter of fact, I did." Berlandier chuckled in response. "I made numerous collections and took many notes of plants, and saw many of the birds and other animals…all observations recorded in my journal of course along with numerous drawings."

"Of course!" Alamán responded, satisfied by the answer,. "That's what I had expected of you when appointed and the need of an observant biologist to report back to this Ministry on everything you do and see to meet our interests."

But while Berlandier felt that his appointment was made principally to be on behalf of the Boundary Commission's needs, he wanted for his own interests to have an opportunity to explore a whole new biota in Mexico and Texas. But at this point he could not have foreseen how much broader his contacts with Native Americans would take him to write of them or put him into dangers when being among them. And that in part would be because his assignment as a botanist/pharmacist was to study the uses of plants by Indians for medicinal purposes. That meant in order to learn of them, he would need to be in their villages amidst them and where and when an outsider was seldom well received.

"Since you asked…and no doubt the reason for your inquiry I have to assume…I *did* observe and make notes of the native peoples."

"Which ones?"

"A diverse bag of them," Berlandier replied, "but it was somewhat to my disappointment not to see any pure-blooded Indians as they seem to be rare about Tampico and along the coast. The people in Tampico are mostly the mixed-blood *costeños* [coastal people] with a dark hue and kinky hair making it obvious that African blood runs in their veins. For the most part they are the fishermen as well as the boatmen who load and unload the ships in port."

Berlandier wrote:

> ["I wish to give here further ideas of these *costeños*. I shall paint in a few words with very somber colors the ways of thee lower classes, and I do no more than report the impressions which are made to me as to appearances, habits, and vices.
>
> "They are not generally handsome although their physiognomy is not at all to be considered disagreeable. Their eyes are black and very impressive. Most of them have very spare beards. Their height is average. And in respect to their character, I found later that the pure indigenes seem to be gentler though more distrustful.
>
> "Among all the people where some degree of civilization exists, there is found a particular class of them called 'rabble' of which a considerable number produce a quite disgusting picture for their laziness. That made a disagreeable effect on me mostly during the first days of my arrival.
>
> "Moreover, murders are so common among the rabble that foreigners would be horrified if it were possible to procure exact statistics for this crime. In the cities and on roads, bands of them as thieves disquiet peaceable citizens."
> (Paraphrased from Berlandier Diary Vol. II Chapter 2)]

"Further up the Pánuco through the Huasteca that you advised me to travel," Berlandier continued, "I found numerous of the Huasteco Indians, though many are already mixed but less like the *costeños* in being more agreeable to look upon and much more industrious. I did find, however, that Huastecans prefer to speak their own dialect and retain their customs rather than adopt those of their Spanish conquerors.

"The more I traveled, however," Berlandier said to continue his observations to Alamán, "I found more pure-blood Indians but also some Negroes and some Sambos [Indians mixed with Africans]. In the more agreeable climates up higher in elevation and deeper into the interior I found quite a large number of whites, among them some

Spaniards still friendly despite the Revolution. But the closer I got to here I saw an ever increasing number of *mestizos* that quite obvious by their countenances are Spaniards mixed with Indians, and I must assume the crosses are with the native Mesoamericans."

"You are quite correct. Most of the *mestizos* are just that."

["I was to learn that most of the Mexican people in the plateau areas about Mexico City are of Asteque and Otomite descent and all are extremely superstitious. While they will seldom pass an image of a saint without at least doffing his hat, the parish priests are convinced that the indigenes secretly worship idols of their superstition beliefs." (Paraphrased from Diary Vol. II Chapter 2)]

"You seem to know already quite a bit about the make-up of our differing people and in particular the indigenes. I gather that you must have studied much about them before coming here."

"I did. I read numerous of Jesuit Paul Le Jeune's seventeenth century writings that as you must know are some of the best sources of information regarding the northern tribes and of France's 1600s endeavors to Christianize…or better said, perhaps, 'civilize' the Indians." Berlandier chuckled. "But also on the long voyage here I had ample bunk time to read James Fenimore Cooper's just published *The Last of the Mohicans* [January of 1826] now very popular in Europe concerning French and British expansions into the New World and subsequent Indian wars."

"I've not yet had an opportunity to read the novel myself though I've read reviews of it to say that despite Cooper's well intended approach to draw sympathy to the plights of the natives, the story is, nevertheless, a very bloody tale of their nature.

"And, yes, I know of Le Jeune's works," Alamán continued, "but unfortunately for us here in Latin America the French worked only with the woodland tribes indigenous to the northern United States and Quebec. Here, of course, the Spanish missionaries worked with the Plains Culture Indians as well as the Mesoamericans but also failed to Christianize many of them. You will see the stone ruins of their

17

failed missions in and around Béjar and elsewhere when you get up into Texas."

Berlandier spoke up to add. "I also studied the explorations of Texas and Mexico by Cabeza de Vaca and Coronado through the 1500s, and much to my interest read of their observations of the Plains Indians. I found it rather amusing that the Spanish explorers spoke of bison as 'cows' and named the Lavaca River after them." Berlandier chuckled.

"You will likely see some large herds of those so-called 'cows' in Texas that we here call 'cibolos,' but they certainly don't look much like the black and white kinds milked around here." Alamán chuckled.

"Nor in France where my family raised and milked Brown Swiss cows, but with regards to the enormous amounts of material on the fauna and flora of Latin America written by von Humboldt, I was most disappointed to read little in his works on the Indians. He did little more than just give rudimentary estimates of their numbers."

"I remember something like about six million that von Humboldt estimated twenty years ago," Alamán remarked, "but I believe that his failure to write much about them was probably attributed to his coming out of the so-called 'Romantic School of Thought.'"

"How so?" Berlandier asked, curiously.

"Well, it's believed that Humboldt considered nature to be perfect until man deformed it...some consider the indigenes to be little more than sub-human deformities...so he neglected to discuss them in his writings. Moreover, Humboldt and others of similar thinking apparently consider that humans in general are unimportant in the purely biological scene."

"Well they certainly are important." Berlandier remarked.

"True! But following the arrival of Europeans in the New World back in the 1500s and 1600s by the Dutch, French, and Spanish, and all back then suffering from such unholy hostilities by the native peoples with no Christian kinds of principles whatsoever, that Natives even today are considered to be unworthy of the Brotherhood of Man. They are still thought that even more by the Anglo-Americans up in Texas as you will soon learn, and much like von Humboldt believing them to be unworthy of human consideration. It was felt by many if not most that the wilder of the natives were and are still utterly incapable of civilized progress beyond the condition in which nature originally placed them.

"And relative to that perception the Europeans who came here from the grand cities of Paris, Rome, and London, and who knew of the great cathedrals, libraries, museums and monuments, found nothing akin or anything even close to the indigenes of their New World environs and cultures. Where Europeans lived in townhouses, mansions, stone castles and marbled palaces, the Indians of the New World lived in mud huts, skin-covered teepees, and brush-made wigwams and wick-i-ups. When the Europeans were making the finest of porcelain china...the most ornate of silverware...and the most beautiful of oil paintings on canvas...the Indians in the New World ate with their fingers from crude clay pots and drew stick-figure pictures on animal hides."

"What you are saying," Berlandier responded "is all well and good for the nomadic tribes and those more sedentary in the northern parts... I've read of all of that...but I've also read about and marveled over pictures of the great cities of the Aztecs and Mayans in these parts and the Incans down in Peru, and read of alphabets, books, calendars, and unbelievable knowledge of mathematics and astronomy with movements of the moon, Venus, and the other planets. And it's well known that the Mesoamericans painted ornate pictures, carved elaborate *stelae,* and constructed magnificent palaces, towering pyramids, and laid out sprawling cities with temples, and plazas and ball courts equal to any of ancient Greece and Egypt."

"I know all of that," Alemán said in response. "I've seen the art and architectural marvels of the Mesoamericans myself, and have written and given lectures on the history of Mexico back to the time of the conquistadores and Spanish conquests. There are as you are pointing out, some very un-comparable differences between the Mesoamericans and those of the north. There are, however, some very comparable comparisons of all of the indigenes whether here or elsewhere."

"Which ones?"

"Well you've already picked up on a major one just during your short tenure here and that being the propensities for superstition. Superstitious beliefs ruled all of everything the Mesoamericans did, and their descendents do still, and all native cultures everywhere with the Gods and idols of their fancies and beliefs.

"Another comparable comparison among all of the aborigines is extreme cruelty and torture to any person not their own or closely allied with them when knowing nothing of anything akin to the Ten Commandments, for example. They know little to nothing of anything morally compassionate or sympathetic, as the Golden Rule and 'love thy neighbor'…for to show any measure of pity is still, to them, a sign of tribal and character weakness.

"But to show signs of tribal strengths," Alamán continued, "another comparison is the incessant never-ending bloody warfare among others of their own color as close to one another as those from one mountain range to another or even from one valley to the next. And in their warring they demonstrate no sympathies to forgive or forget, only to exact revenge. That, simply, is just the inherent nature of them going back for eons. They know no other ways.

"If you're ready and willing for the challenges, even dangers of traveling amongst them, there are at least twenty or more tribes just in Coahuila y Tejas that you may soon encounter and be hostile. We are going to send you to San Antonio de Béxar via Monterrey and Laredo to as best we can keep you out of the ranges of the Lipan and Mescalero Apache tribes in the western parts of Texas and as far south into Chihuahua. But it will be unavoidable to keep you out of the ranges of the Comanche in and around Béxar and much of Texas and south to Monterrey who *can* be friendly *when* it behooves them but more often are not peaceful.

"But once in Béxar you will be working closely with Colonel José Francisco Ruiz, a former Mexican army officer who will be your principle informant on the Comanches and their allies and enemies. He has lived with and about them for eight years now and is well accepted by them almost as if he were one of their own. He speaks their language fluently and can be an interpreter for your needs. With Colonel Ruiz close by at all times you may be able to study the people with little interference… at least less of it…but they may be more tolerant of you out of curiosity than actually be friendly. But even when with Ruiz, be suspicious at all times of anything the Comanches do as while they may seem friendly in pretense one day they will turn on you the next."

"Who will be going with me…certainly not by myself? Berlandier asked with some concern.

"Oh no!" Alamán chuckled. "Don't worry. You and the Commission will be escorted by a military detachment of dragoons from here in

Mexico City. Brigadier General Manuel Mier y Terán appointed by the President himself is well qualified to lead the expedition into frontier areas. He fought in the war for independence from Spain and is well experienced in military matters. Moreover, you will likely find the General convenient to your assistance in the field as he is also quite knowledgable in the natural sciences and in mathematics and engineering. Terán is the most scientific man in the Mexican army. I know him well, having been a fellow student with him in the Mexico School of Mines."

"Will there be any others to go with us?" Berlandier asked, curiously.

"Yes, Rafael Chowel who is presently here in the School of Mines will serve as mineralogist. He is about your same age and will be a good friend and traveling companion. Lieutenant José María Sánchez y Tapia will serve as cartographer as well as a writer to report findings. Lieutenant Colonel José Batres will be a medical officer and Lieutenant Colonel Constantino Tarnava will serve as an engineer.

"While the mission is primarily for scientific purposes and to define questionable boundaries, you need to be made aware that an underlying though major reason for the Commission led by a General trained in geology is to also collect geographical information of rivers and streams and of their courses, and the locations of the Anglo-American inhabitants in case of a possible conflict with them who already talk of separating from Coahuila and are seeking closer relations with the United States.

"Texas is already slipping from the grasp of Mexico, and settlers keep pouring across the border without permission of authorities and who already have possession of practically all of the eastern part of Texas. Moreover, the combined American and European immigrants outnumber Mexican nationals twenty to one and the President wants to encourage increasing numbers of Mexicans into the region.

"Furthermore, he wants Terán to assess the political situations, wealth, and sentiments of the populace in order to make recommendations for ways to close the boundaries between Texas and the United States. He wants no more Americans to come into the country. And, too, the President wants to know more about the ports and navigation of the rivers for future needs, and to provide for closer trade ties between the existing Texans and Mexico. Still more, it will be the responsibility of the Commission to obtain data on the customs, dispositions, and habits of the native tribes, as well as estimates of their numbers and of any willingness to side with Mexican troops in case of a revolution."

"But I am French…not Mexican…and little do I yet speak much of either Spanish or English. All of my correspondence and journals will necessarily be in French. So what role can I possibly play in such interests?"

"Observe and note what you can of the land and peoples. Talk with the Anglo-Americans as best you can and especially with the Indians. Some tribes do speak some English but more speak Spanish from a long history of contact with Spanish explorers and conquerors. Some Indians do, believe it or not, speak a bit of French from communication early on with French traders and clerics but you will likely find it being hard to understand their French pronunciations in their native 'speak.'" Alamán laughed. "But of any and all information that you can acquire in talking with them make it available to us here including duplicate specimens and records of your collections."

"Well that I plan to do anyway according to the agreements made between you and De Candolle before my coming here, but where along the way can I ship specimens to Geneva?"

"Terán plans I believe to be in the port village of Matamoros on the Rio Bravo near the end of his expedition in Texas before returning here. You can ship from there all that you have collected by then, or arrange for shipments to be transported first to New Orleans and then from there on one of the vessels occasionally sailing for Le Havre."

[A shipment of four large cases to A. P. De Candolle in Geneva was shipped from New Orleans in April, 1829, containing 216 pages of records and 184 lots of herbarium and zoological specimens and seeds. Each lot was serially numbered including the names, both Latin and vernacular, if known, and the localities of origin. Other shipments of two cases were shipped out of Tampico in April, 1827, soon after Berlandier's arrival in Mexico, and three cases were shipped out of Matamoros in November, 1830, and July, 1831. A count of *all* specimens shipped by then from

Berlandier numbered 52,000 dried plants and respectable numbers of seeds and animals.]

According to Geiser, Berlandier *did* visit New Orleans between April 25 and May 5, 1829—the April date when his specimens were shipped—aboard the galette *Pomona*, and Geiser remarked: "It is evident that Berlandier loved the French people of New Orleans and parted with them with profound regret." Fatigued by the monotony of a semi-savage life and of ignorance and superstition, Berlandier himself wrote of his New Orleans visit:

["I found among the people, descendents of our ancestors, the urbanity, the *soins prévenances*, the benevolence, freedom, and the gayety which will always be the lasting characteristics of this unhappy nation, by all men (meaning principally the French) considered the most civilized on our planet.")]

Chapter Four
THE JOURNEY INTO TEXAS

The Boundary Commission appointed to explore the lands north into Texas left Mexico City on the tenth of November, 1827, after two months of preparations for the journey had been completed. However, many stops were needed along the entire route to repair breakdowns of wheels on the two mule drawn wagons. One was for basic supplies but the other was especially equipped and padded for the safety of instruments including three types of thermometers, two barometers, compasses, telescopes, a sextant and a chronometer. In addition was the all-important collecting equipment of plant presses, drying papers, jars with preserving alcohol, and the indispensable maps and reference books including texts on the physical and natural sciences. But not the least of the wheeled vehicles subject to breakdowns was the oversized carriage for General Terán.

Just on the following day, on the eleventh, it was already necessary to repair a wheel on the instrument wagon as well as within to replace tubes in a barometer broken from the jostling of rough road travel. The padding was obviously insufficient to the needs and only on the twelfth another wheel on the same wagon broke. Then, after only another twelve days of travel an axle on the supply wagon broke once again, and while a new one was replaced on the spot it was only a bit further that same day that another wheel fell off in pieces. Berlandier wrote:

> ["Roads all along the way were hardly passable for wheeled vehicles without risking spills and some of the roads were virtually impassable. The government of Mexico scarcely bothers itself with the betterment of its roads, and the wheels of our wagons broke one after another." (Paraphrased from Berlandier Diary Vol. III Chapter 2)]

Following a cross-country route "ever so slow and punishing" the expedition reached the ill-defined border of southern Coahuilla y Texas and the capital villa of Saltillo in late December.

["The inhabitants of that capital have a bad reputation involving crimes which in any other country would lead the perpetrators to the gallows, but they continually escape punishments imposed by law because of their kinship with the authorities who judge them. To be born in Saltillo (to be a *Saltillero*) is a black mark in the country." (From Berlandier's Diary Vol. III Chapter 4)]

On more of the same miserable roads crossed by innumerable watercourses and being so indistinct and unmarked—and with poor directions given by the locals—the party was continually in doubt of the correct road to get there but eventually arrived in Monterrey, the destination, on the seventh of January, 1828, and there stayed for two weeks.

["Most of the people in Monterrey out of a population of about 12,000 are Creoles; the lower classes of them composed of indigenes of whom most are mixed with Negroes or mulattoes. But early-on in the history of Monterrey, others had long ago retreated into the wilderness where their villages presently are."

Of animals of the area, Berlandier wrote of reptiles, and fish in the waters, and took special note of "small fish found in a very dark cavern that sufficiently proved that light must not be the only coloring agent of them for these animals which have no exposures to lighted places have a very deep color." (Paraphrased from Berlandier Diary Vol. III Chapter 5)]

On the twenty-first of January the expedition continued ever so slowly for Texas via an ill-defined route to the villa of Salinas Victoria, though *en route* the breakdowns of wagon wheels were continuously troublesome. The population in the villa of about 2500 was found to be engaged mostly in agriculture or in the manufacture of blankets used as *serapes*. Berlandier wrote:

["Warring indigenes sometimes appear in the vicinity and I have been told that Lipan Apaches when committing their depredations descend from hills about the town. But whether at peace or war the Lipans prevent the inhabitants from raising herds and dedicating themselves freely to farming." (Paraphrased from Berlandier Diary Vol. III Chapter 5)]

The next day the expedition continued but at times lost its way in ravines amidst dense forests of mimosa and other trees.

["The vehicles made but slow progress as they followed the military escort which was opening a passage. A small tribe of Indians called Carrizos, one of the most wretched of tribes, was living of the banks of a stream in the shade of the forest, and the camp was ten or twelve huts built of palm fronds. The inhabitants evidently prefer idleness for they are indolent and rarely seek work from nearby haciendas. Dress among the men consists of a body covering in winter, but in summer wear only a square scrap of cotton cloth over their genitals. The women in summertime wear a dress only from the waist to the knees.

"They greatly fear the Comanche who exterminate all of whom they encounter. In winter when the Comanche come to the area the Carrizos draw close to inhabited places for some measure of protection.

"In times of war with the indigenes it is dangerous to travel over these roads, which fearfully recall the numerous cruelties that the Lipans and Comanches perpetrate. Men working in the fields are sometimes murdered, and when one night just last year Comanches attacked eight shepherds who were gathering in their flocks. All but one was massacred and from him it was told that one of the other shepherds had hidden in a thicket but was betrayed by the barking of his dog. The shepherd was found and killed on the spot." (Paraphrased from Berlandier's Diary Vol. III Chapter 5)]

By the second of February, 1828, the expedition finally reached the Rio Bravo del Norte (aka Rio Grande) and the border town of Laredo, a distance of more than 700 miles taking 84 days or twelve weeks, or about 8 miles per day on average of slow and punishing travel. But "roads" over most of the way were little more than ill-defined tracks, and the numerous breakdowns of wheels and axels had much hindered speed of the progress. Moreover at times, "almost step by step" the soldier escorts needed their sabers to cut brush and widen tracks little accustomed to the travel of wagons. To the hardships of all was the oppressive heat even in the months of January and February.

["The country was as arid as during the previous days and the plains that stretched before our eyes seemed to be on fire from the heat, and in spite of our utmost care our water gave out because of the heat and we suffered considerable from thirst. This became even more unbearable as there wasn't a single tree under which we might rest in shade. But, finally, we discerned in the distance the peaceful waters of the Rio Bravo del Norte lying like a silver thread upon the immensity of the plains.

"The desires to reach quickly the water made our last way more anxious and arduous and when like us that the beasts fatigued by their own thirst were scarcely able to make another step we arrived at the coveted stream." (Sánchez, *A Trip To Texas in 1828*)]

["On exploring the banks of the river, we encountered the huts and debris of the chase of some wandering tribe which had lived there a short time ago. Even when there is peace with these tribes, the indigenes come here to plunder the village and rob travelers being only too happy if escaping so lightly.

"We crossed over at once with most crossing on horseback since the water was only about four feet deep in its deepest places." (Paraphrased from Berlandier's Diary Vol. III Chapter 5)]

Notes: Fording the Rio Bravo del Norte by wheeled vehicles over a shallow sandstone bottom was likely easy, compared to the long heretofore traveling of narrow rocky roads described in Berlandier's diary. And while Berlandier infers kindly of his toleration of the large oversized carriage used privately by General Terán—who he ardently admired—he spoke little of it. But its widely spaced wheels were no doubt serious problems causing the frequent uses of sabers to "cut brush and to widen tracks." The numerous mentions of "wagon" breakdowns by Berlandier were likely, though not said, more those of the carriage.

But rank has its privileges, and all others in the Border Commission rode horseback when on the march and with lesser protection from the elements than the General in his carriage.

An unbiased fair-minded description of the carriage was however given by an American who saw it in or near to San Felipe, Texas, and such elaboration suggests the problems experienced on narrow roads.

["The General's coach was a remarkable and indescribable machine of a prodigious size two or three feet wider than normal. It was constructed of huge pieces of timber much carved, inlaid and plated with silver. The rear wheels were large and the front wheels were little superior than those of a wheelbarrow." (Paraphrased from J.C. Clopper)]

Berlandier does, however, mention the broken "carriage" when on arrival in Laredo he wrote:

["During our short stay, having need of wood to repair our carriage, we were obliged to send soldiers to cut it on the banks of the Nueces River, the closest locality where wood could be found in the quality needed (likely oak)." (Paraphrased from Berlandier's Diary Vol. III Chap. 6)]

Laredo area trees and/or lack of them are described by Berlandier as "miserable" as he "saw no trees for a distance of more than fifty leagues suitable for any kind of construction. Only willows, huisache, and mesquites comprised the higher trees though the ground was covered with evergreen shrubbery, that principally of cenizo [desert sage]."

Of the river animals, Berlandier wrote of beavers and otters, and of gars, catfish, eels and perches as well as freshwater shrimp and shellfish, but found it strange that there were no alligators in the Rio Bravo when common in other Texas rivers as near to the north as the Nueces.

Chapter Five
THE STREETS OF LAREDO

The villa de San Agustín de Laredo, or the Presidio of Laredo, belonged to the State of Tamaulipas, and in Berlandier's time the streets were quite wide and paved with bricks to the credit of Spanish founders. The population in 1827 numbered only about 2,000, apart from the presidio company of about 100 soldiers stationed there to protect the villa from raids by Lipans and Comanches. Such depredations started after arrival of the Comanches down from the north in the mid-1700s [Laredo founded in 1755] and soon began raiding the villa and murdering priests and parishioners and abducting girls and young women of childbearing ages for slaves, concubines, and for propagation purposes.

["Laredo is no more than a village with the title of villa that before the stationing of troops much exposed to attacks by the indigenes but mostly now only subjected to their annoyance as beggars, thieves, idlers and drunkards. They cannot be enticed into the mission for salvation because work is expected of the men. The two tribes that most frequent Laredo are the Lipans and the Comanches who come to camp on the banks of the river. Since the two tribes have been at war, the Lipans are always there to be protected from the Comanches. There are some Carrizos who also fear the Comanches and seek protection from them.

"The inhabitants of Laredo are of mixed blood; several families are very white while many others have some indigenous blood. Although not very hardworking or industrious, many are in military service. Some are muleteers, others are laborers, or are farmers and shepherds. The houses are not at all remarkable as the majority of them are nothing but thatch-covered huts although evenly distributed along evenly spaced streets and blocks of one hundred square varas including two plazas though without

31

verdure. The founding Spaniards never seemed to get the idea of planting trees." (Paraphrased from Berlandier's Diary Vol. III Chapter 6)]

History records that special assignments of the presidios were to war on the hostile tribes and to defend villagers from raids along the northern boundary of the Republic. The presidios were established at strategic places and during his time in Texas Berlandier visited back and forth between those at San Agustín de Laredo, San Antonio de Béxar, and La Bahia (Goliad) where in the areas Berlandier also made many of his richest collections. But Berlandier wrote poorly of his presidios:

["The presidio soldiers are poor at fighting the savages, much less than the mounted cavalry but are detailed to watch the movements of the natives at peace or on the warpath, and to protect any frontier populations from native depredations. They are also in charge of the security of the roads that lead to the presidios and provide armed escorts for the convoys that travel from one to another." (Paraphrased from Berlandier *The Indians of Texas in 1830*)]

Of observations of the Indians Berlandier wrote:

["The arrival of natives at a frontier presidio is a special occasion. The people are always glad to see them when in peace since the government pays the civilians a percentage of the trade profits. Moreover, their visits are assurance that the visiting tribe is not, for a time, being hostile.

"When I was in Béxar in September, 1828, several large groups of natives from the large Comanche nation came to visit the presidio. As many as two or three hundred of these natives arrived, bringing their wives and children. Whenever they came like this, bringing their offspring, the visit was a visible proof of peace, of friendship and trust; whereas if they had only a few women with them (who could also be hostile combatants) it was because they were at war.

"When such natives approach a presidio, they make camp a league away and send a courier with notice of their arrival and a request for permission to enter. The garrison troops mount and go out to escort them in and the entry then becomes very pompous and processional. As the bugles sound you can see all the natives holding themselves very proudly, riding between the ranks of cavalry drawn up with sabers flashing in salute. I once witnessed such a group of Comanches take umbrage when no escort went to meet them and this slight was enough to make them decide not to enter the presidio at all.

"When two tribes who are at war with each other meet in a presidio or in the vicinity, they are forbidden to fight except at a considerable distance. In 1828 when the party of Comanches I was speaking of was encamped in the main square of Béxar, the Lipans who were at war with them at the time came close to the town, and in the night the chiefs went secretly to the garrison leader, asking for permission to attack them. The Comanches learning of Lipan presence folded their blankets and fled in haste being fearful of a larger force of the enemy at the time. The Lipans pursued them more than thirty leagues (approximately 90 miles) from Béxar to the banks of the Colorado where the Lipans then stole more than two hundred horses without killing a single Comanche because the Comanches had a defensible position in a ravine." (Paraphrased from Berlandier *The Indians of Texas in 1830*)

["The Lipan Apaches, southernmost of the numerous Apache tribes, then lived south of the Comanche and in the neighborhood of the Rio Grande. They were traditional enemies of the Comanche who had driven them from more favorable territory." (John C. Ewers, Editor's notation).]

Chapter Six
ON TO SAN ANTONIO DE BÉXAR

The more northerly that the Boundary Commission traveled, the more mixed were its feelings and fears. The beauty of the land was striking. The brightest of clear day suns illuminated the most beautiful of landscapes dressed in the most vivid of colors with backgrounds of evergreen oaks and other trees. Large herds of wild horses and buffalo and deer were sometimes seen in the distance but there was also the very real likelihood of seeing bands of marauding Indians somewhere along the way, principally the Lipan and/or Mescalero Apaches but the more feared would be Comanches or their allies the Tahuacanos, both tribes well known already as terrors of the plains.

["The Tahuacanos and Comanches have the reputation of being the most sensuous, pleasure-loving natives in Texas. Their women seldom repulse the advances of admirers, and the corrupt men of this tribe give themselves over to the (bestial) satisfaction of all their indecent passions with all the animals, domestic or wild.

"Some of this tribe is guilty of murder and/or horse stealing around the Texas presidios where they are greatly feared. On one occasion some of them stole my horse and those of the five dragoons who were my escort only a few leagues outside Béxar." (Paraphrased from Berlandier's *The Indians of Texas in 1830*)]

Berlandier and the numerous others of the Boundary Commission including the armed escort rode on into San Fernando de Béxar. Two plazas—Main and Military—in the center of town almost joined one another and the river that flowed through the villa further divided the town. Opposite Military Plaza stood the white-washed adobe-made home of Colonel José Francisco Ruiz who commanded the Alamo de Parras company at the presidio, and who was to become Berlandier's principal informant on the Comanche Indians and their allies including the aforementioned Tahuacanos.

But long into his experiences with Texas Indians including eight years with the Comanches Ruiz wrote a "Report on the Indian Tribes of Texas" in 1818, and during his many years in the military Ruiz gained confidences of the Indians as a negotiator referred to by the Shawnees as "A good man no lie and a friend of the Indian's." It was with the Comanches that Ruiz was named a "commissioner" in attempts to keep them friendly and why Lucas Alamán as Minister of Foreign Affairs advised Berlandier to contact Ruiz on arrival in Béxar. "He knows the tribe intimately and speaks their language fluently." Alamán confided.

Ruiz exited the front door of his home upon hearing the contingent arriving in the distance with the sounds of a bugle, and then the ringing of the San Fernando Cathedral bell plus the heralding barking of sentinel dogs. Ruiz had for days, already, anticipated their arrival with advance news sent by a courier up from Laredo on their arrival there, and weeks before by letters from Minister Alamán.

"*Hola y buenos tardes*" Ruiz called out to them all. Berlandier and the others almost in unison bid a "*hola y buenos tardes*" in return as they rode closer, then dismounted with additional salutations and introductions by all. Plans were made immediately to billet the military escort at the presidio where Ruiz was a commanding officer, and at Ruiz's insistence Berlandier and his now good friend Rafael Chowell opted to stay as guests with Ruiz. General Terán and Lieutenant Colonels Batres and Tarnava quartered with General Anastacio Bustamente, then military commander of all of the Internal Provinces and who at the time was residing in Béxar at the governmental *palacio*. [In 1830 Bustamente became President of Mexico.]

Seated inside the comfort of Ruiz's home with a *cerveza* each ordered at once from nearby Black's Saloon, and with the sweet smells of mountain laurels wafting in through opened shutters from off the backyard gardens, Berlandier and Chowell brought Ruiz up-to-date on their travels. Much to Ruiz's interests were the encounters with Carrizos south of the border, but in keeping abreast of Indian depredations region-wide Ruiz knew already about the murders of shepherds by Comanches and Lipans near Salinas Victoria.

["Murder is such a matter of complete indifference among the natives and unless against their friends and relations murder actually improves their standings in the tribes. Unfortunately, there are examples of murders committed by the natives even in times of peace with the victims being of other natives or even the inhabitants of the presidios who when suspecting no harm might find themselves threatened by them. This penchant for murder among the natives stems from the facts that all by their nature are vindictive, treacherous, and untrustworthy even to their own, fickle in friendships, and with an active taste for killing and even torturing most anything that breathes." (Paraphrased from Berlandier's *The Indians of Texas in 1830*)

"Cruelty among Indians is an inherent amusement and of such pleasure that an Indian is constantly thinking of new ways of torture." (Col. Richard Irving Dodge, U.S. Army)

"The pleasure to the Indian when torturing prisoners was unquestionable, and that cruelty was early manifested by the young who tortured birds, turtles, or any other small animal that might fall into their hands. They delighted in it." (Fanny Kelley, Sioux captive)]

"Do you know where you are going from here?" Ruiz asked, curiously. "I've heard all the way to the border with the Territory of Louisiana and the United States."

"The President and Alamán" Chowell answered, "want us to proceed eastward as far as Nacogdoches on the Sabine. And I believe Terán plans to go through Gonzales and San Felipe de Austin en route which as you probably know the Anglo-Americans are fast settling in much of that part of central Texas."

Berlandier spoke up to add to the answer that "The President wants to know the current sentiments of the settlers who swore allegiance to Mexico in order to settle in Texas, but are talking already of splitting off from Coahuilla y Tejas as a separate State. Beyond that I'm...we're... not sure just yet of when and where exactly we'll be going, but we *will* be returning here to Béxar and on to Goliad, and ultimately south to Matamoros where I will need to ship my plant collections off to Switzerland for De Candolle's needs."

"Well, then, that may put you back here by late summer and if by then you are up to the opportunity," Ruiz chuckled, "I can probably arrange for us to participate in a buffalo and bear hunt with the Comanches."

"We wouldn't have thought that you had such good relationships with them." Chowell remarked with some concern. "All along the way here we've heard only of troubles with the Comanches even as far south as Monterrey...with raids and abductions and all...and just days ago we learned that south of the border the Carrizos move closer to neighboring haciendas for some measures of protection from Comanche raids."

> ["For a long time we had been desirous of exploring the western parts of Texas beyond Béxar where silver mines are reported but because of an insecure peace with the savages—a peace which was often interrupted suddenly by hostilities—the Boundary Commission did not dare visit those little known regions. It had been about a year since the Comanches had signed a peace treaty but only a few groups of the Comanches had yet come to trade in the markets." (Paraphrased from Berlandier's Vol. IV Chapter 4)]

"Well as you may know, I've lived here for some twenty-five years already since first becoming a school teacher, then joining the Béxar Provincial Militia to help make peace with the Indians...at least some measure of it." Ruiz chuckled. "For eight years I essentially lived with them to gain their confidences but can't promise you with certainty if there will still be peace with the Comanches for a buffalo hunt when you return.

"They are fickle in their friendships as they can be amiable one day but not the next and with little to no knowledge of what or will put them on the warpath again. But I have maintained some rather good relations with the Comanche chief Keiuna, and especially with Barbakista who still honors bonds of amity with Texans." [However, on March 19, 1840, just twelve years later, the "Council House Fight" between Comanches and Texans on the corner of Main Plaza and Market Street in Béxar with the death of Chief Muguara and eleven other Comanche chiefs ended the truce for the remainder of the Texas frontier history thus resulting in a soon-to-happen Comanche vengeance raid on Linnville resulting in the subsequent Plum Creek battle that was a great defeat of the Comanches. (Brice)]

"What can we expect in the way of troubles with any of the other tribes en route to Nacogdoches?" Berlandier asked, curiously. "You've been there yourself."

"In fact I just returned from there through San Felipe and Gonzales along the newly established Béxar to San Felipe Road, though it isn't much of a road being marked in some places only with flags and blazes on tree trunks," Ruiz chuckled. "But during rains the so-called road is little more than one long quagmire.

"But as for Indians along the way you will no doubt encounter the Tancahuesas [Tonkawas] between the Guadalupe and Colorado Rivers and across the Lavaca and Navidad. Until recently they were hostile to Americans but now friendly since finding settlers as an outlet for their trading goods, and good allies against mutual enemies, principally the Comanches. The Tancahuesas are bitter enemies with them.

"Beyond the Colorado and east and south to Matamoros you may encounter the Kickapoos along the Trinity near Nacogdoches, and perhaps some Caddos and no doubt Cherokees if you venture north of there. They are abundant along the Sabine, and you will likely encounter the Karankawas and their Cocos allies along the coast and the Aranamas around Goliad on your way back…as well as more Carrizos and Lipan Apaches between Matamoros and Laredo if you return that route." (See **Frontispiece** Map for tribe locations)

"Are there anymore for God's sake?" Berlandier responded with some expression of surprise of so many tribes mentioned.

"Isn't that enough?" Ruiz replied, amused by the remark. "But I should add that any of the Indians you may encounter can be deceitful and treacherous…or friendly when and if it behooves them…so always be suspicious of their activities and intents. It's just the way that they are. The Comanches, Tahuacanos and Lipans when hostile can and will pretend friendships to catch you off guard, and watch after your horses carefully or they'll get stolen." Ruiz laughed.

"How long do you expect to be here in Béxar?" Ruiz asked.

"We think until about mid-April, but we're not for sure just yet as there are some things we want to do around here." Chowell replied.

"I hope that the some of those things" Ruiz smiled with a wry grin, and said more in jest, "is to enjoy the festivities while here and the *señoritas* are quite pretty."

"Well them, too, of course" Berlandier remarked with a chuckle. "But we need to collect area plants and minerals in order to keep our jobs with the Commission." All laughed.

"I should add, though, a bit more about the *señoritas*." Ruiz interjected. "They commonly marry young, about the age of fifteen when they celebrate their coming-of-age, the *quinceaneras* festivities. All are chaperoned long before marriage of course, according to custom, but an occasional sympathetic aunt or big sister sometimes pay less attention to what goes on between a young girl and her *novio* in the next room." Both Berlandier and Chowell in their early and viral twenties grinned in response to such a scenario.

Also in Béxar in 1828, the following is given of a young American man's observations and opinions (paraphrased).

["Though not fully understanding their language I did form an acquaintance with two or three families and am received well by them. I became somewhat a favorite with a landlady who has two daughters and I accompanied them several times to the festivities, waltzes, fandangos and reels, always performed in the streets.

"Men do not select their partners, this being left to the ladies. But the men first place themselves in a line, and when the latter arise and face the subjects of their choice it sometimes happens that two or more of the young ladies make the same selection and then there is a good deal of elbowing among the fair sexes.

"There are always chaperones since unmarried girls are diligently kept from being alone with the other sex, unless one of their parents is present to keep watch of what's going on. But as soon as married, the girls are scarcely the same creatures, giving the freest indulgence to their enthusiasms as if liberated from all moral constraints." ("J.C. Clopper's Journal And Book of Memoranda For 1828")]

Berlandier wrote much less of such, other than to comment, paraphrased:

[“On the thirteenth of April we departed regretfully from Ciudad de Béxar which had been a restful and fun-filled sojourn with all of the many festivities, and the inhabitants who received us very well.” (Berlandier's Diary Vol. IV Chapter 2)]

Notes: The following is paraphrased from John C. Ewers, Editor of Berlandier's *The Indians of Texas in 1830*.

[During the month and a half that he was in San Antonio, Berlandier made extensive botanical collections and became interested in the Comanche, the largest and most feared tribe of Texas. Only the previous year General Bustamente had negotiated a tenuous peace with that portion of the tribe living nearest to San Antonio, and these Indians visited the town to trade buffalo hides and meat, and bear grease for guns and ammunition, and other goods as pots, pans and trinkets manufactured by whites.]

Chapter Seven
ON TO GONZALES

After leaving the Villa de Béxar and following the so-called "Middle Road" between Béxar and San Felipe to the east, the Boundary Commission camped its first night at the Arroyo de Salado [Stream of Salty Water] seven leagues (about twenty-one miles) from its point of departure. And, there, Berlandier made collections and notes of bluish lupines [bluebonnets], amid pinkish primroses and purplish verbenas that "contrasted with the greens of the grasses from which sprang the many flowers of various colors." Berlandier made mention of oaks, elms, sycamores, and pecan trees; then wrote of a major concern:

["I heard it said in Béxar that the Salado area is infested with warring indigenes who too often commit murders there. But during the night we heard nothing but the lowing of the *Rana taurina* (bullfrog, aka *Rana catesbiana*); the cries of the Texas screech owl; and that of a species of cuckoo." (Paraphrased from Berlandier's diary Vol. IV Chapter 2)]

["The members of our party kept watch for fear of an attack by the Indians who abound through this area. There we heard for the first time the frog with a call that resembles the bellowing of a bull. Though rarely seen, the croaking by its monotony and melancholy does not fail in the silence of night to arouse sadness." (Paraphrased from Sanchez *A Trip to Texas in 1828)*]

The road over which the Commission traveled was first established by the Mexicans to connect Béxar with Gonzales on the Guadalupe River and then by Anglo-Americans as far as San Felipe on the Colorado to become known in 1828 as the Gonzales to San Felipe Road, but *en route* to also cross Peach Creek and the Lavaca and Navidad Rivers. Between the Salado and Cibolo arroyos three Americans from Gonzales were encountered *en route* to Béxar with two wagonloads of pecans harvested on the banks of the Guadalupe. The Commission moved on ever slowly with the further observations:

["The beauty of the countryside along the way was so constant that even the road itself was covered with flowers. On the prairies are observed ranunculi, vetches, salvias, and occasional chelones (turtles and tortoises, but likely the Texas tortoise, *Gopherus berlanderia* (**Plate 4**). In the midst of the leas we saw old oaks surrounded with saplings from their acorns, beginning to form small forests together with its progeny (a mot or motte). At other times the mezquite (mesquite) formed separate groups not mixing with other vegetation.

"As one nears to the Guadalupe the countryside is covered with low lying hills which form undulations everywhere and we soon found the tranquil waters of the Guadalupe River at the bottom of a deep ravine, its edges thronged with trees. Many fish and alligators are found there, and on the left bank an Indian village probably belonging to the Tancahueses (Tonkawas) had been abandoned. The rounded conical-shaped huts were about five feet high and made of tree branches. Everything indicated a temporary camp, perhaps to be reused at other times. The few inhabitants of Gonzales came to ferry our baggage across in a sort of ferry boat formed by the joining of two *pirogues* (canoes)." (Paraphrased from Berlandier's diary Vol. IV Chapter 2)]

The Villa de Gonzales described by Berlandier was comprised of "six cabins built on the eastern bank in addition to others isolated and scattered here and there in the forest." The few families comprising the newly established DeWitt Colony raise some corn and cotton along with bullocks, cows, pigs and fowl as sources of subsistence, and some horses, but all of the people live in much fear of attacks by hostile Comanches, Lipan Apaches, and Carancahuese that roam through the region in pursuit of buffalo, and their hostilities make living in Gonzales dangerous.

One of the settlers was a very pretty young girl, age about ten, feared for her safety by Lt. José María Sánchez y Tapia [a writer member of the Commission] from knowledge of Comanche depredations infamous in Texas and Mexico for abductions of girls and young women of breeding age. With that fear for the young girl in mind, Lt. Sánchez wrote:

["On the eastern bank of the Guadalupe there are six wooden cabins, and inhabited with the men there are two women and two girls. One of the girls barely more than ten years-old and whose beauty made her attractive came out to offer me a chair to sit with that charming grace that only innocence can lend. Her kindness and the sight of her rose-like face and bare little feet, and the knowledge of human misery which at the moment plagued my mind moved me rather strangely.

I thought that perhaps someday tears would come to the face of this flower of a child where joy and smiles now dwell. These fearful thoughts for her permitted me only to thank her for her kindness, and I returned to my camp to wait for slumber to come and deaden the bitter thoughts of the afternoon of what may lay in the future for such a pretty girl if ever abducted." (Paraphrased from Lt. José María Sánchez y Tapia, *A Trip To Texas In 1828*)]

Note: According to information given by Sharon Anne Dobyns Moehring author of *The Gonzales Connection*, the young girl was Eveline DeWitt (1817-1891) who was a daughter of empresario Green DeWitt and who in 1828 would have been ten years-old as Sánchez had estimated her age and who lived to be 74 years-old.]

Chapter Eight
ENCOUNTER WITH THE TANCAHUESES

Berlandier, Chowell, Sánchez and others of the entourage under the leadership of General Terán continued northeasterly from Gonzales *en route* to San Felipe de Austin on the Colorado but with difficulties to follow the little traveled route barely visible being overgrown already with lush new growths of grasses and the many varieties of colorful spring flowers as further described.

["The road runs through rolling country covered with woods, and the meadows we met from time to time present to the eye all of the beauty of wild nature. The countryside bedecked with beautiful flowers where numerous butterflies flitted about made the solitary regions all the more charming. And when one inhales the perfumes of the many flowers and listens to the singing of birds, the soul seems to revel in unknown joy." (Paraphrased from Lt. José María Sánchez y Tapia, *A Trip To Texas In 1828*)]

["We passed through pretty prairies so beautifully interrupted with trees that I lack words to describe them. They were fields of flowers of an exquisite variety not only in their varied colors but also because of the forms that nature had given them. It is difficult for me to explain the joy that I felt from its enchantment.

"The trees that grew along the rivers and creeks take great pride in reaching immense heights to form domes, and in the passing beneath them it is a delightful experience for the traveler and where the heart is moved.

"But what makes these woods even more delightful, it is the wide variety of birds inhabiting them of which their trills and warbling give a greater animation to nature already overflowing with life and beauty." (Paraphrased from José Enrique de la Peña *With Santa Anna in Texas; A Personal Narrative of the Revolution* written in 1836)]

It was only within the past year that the route between Gonzales and San Felipe had been surveyed by Captain James Kerr in order to provide DeWitt colonists on the Guadalupe access to San Felipe on the Brazos, the then center of government of the Stephen F. Austin Colony. Through wooded areas, direction of the route was marked only with blazes on tree trunks and with stakes and flags across prairies, though at times the latter were still difficult to follow. Mounted soldiers always scouting ahead for signs of Indians, and sitting high in saddles, still lost sights of markers in taller grasses with needs at times to track back to relocate the ill-defined road.

When surveying its route, Captain Kerr approached the banks of most rivers by following dry creek beds already channeled down to river levels by erosion that functioned for the best if only practical approaches down to rivers. (*Fig. 3* The Gonzales to San Felipe Road following a dry creek bed down to the Lavaca River).

["Halfway between Béxar and San Felipe we crossed the Lavaca River but only with great difficulty for the slope still retained a steep gradient." (From Berlandier's diary Vol. IV Chapter 2)]

Berlandier wrote that it was there [believed to have been at the above Lavaca River crossing] when the party was forced to stop and camp for a day until repairs of another broken wheel could be made.

Wherever they made camps, soldier sentries always watched for Indians, often hostile though usually wary of attacking a well-armed force as was the Boundary Commission with some thirty mounted soldiers for protection. From the top of a tall tree used for a vantage point a lookout spotted an indigene and called down his presence to the attention of Berlandier, Chowell, and Sánchez who were much interested in native Indians. Berlandier wrote of the incident:

["He was an old Indian of the Tancahueses (Tonkawa) tribe who lived in a neighboring village about four miles to the west of our encampment. The old man was near seventy years old and his whole body was in a state of decrepitude, and he made us understand that he was overcome by hunger. Someone gave him biscuits and some scraps of dried meat which he carried off with care. On his brow he bore the scars of a wound received from the Comanches; it was probably from a spent ball which had made a cavity half the size of its caliber in one of the frontal bones. He was in the greatest of want, without arms, without a horse, without any of the ornaments of savage luxury. He was almost naked except that his genitals were hidden under a chamoised pronghorn hide. A scrap of leather served him as a belt and he wore that same type of leather as footgear known as *teguas* (moccasins) made of buckskin." (Paraphrased from Berlandier's diary Vol. IV Chapter 2)]

Lt. Sánchez added additional information to the story:

["His skin was closely attached to his bones. His deep wrinkles made it evident that he was burdened by seventy or eighty years of age and that the grave was calling him. Learning that his camp was not far Messrs Batres, Chowell, and Berlandier immediately left to see them and returned at nightfall with the chief of the tribe and other members of it.

"Moved by the curiosity about what my traveling companions said about the camp of the Tancahuesas, it was I and the general who went to see it, situated in the center of a thick grove. All came out to see us and while the general talked to the chief of the tribe, I examined the Indians about whom I obtained much information. Their huts were small, barely numbering thirty, and all were conical in shape, made with light branches covered with the same material and an occasional buffalo skin. In the center of each is located the fireplace around which the male Indians are in complete inaction, while the women are in constant motion either curing the meat of the game or tanning the skin or preparing the food which consists chiefly of roast meat, or perhaps making weapons for the indolent husbands. The women work hard though the younger of them have times of rest (?) at the expense of the wretched men elders who enjoy their presence.

"The tribe is small in number but they are brave friends of the Lipans and other tribes found in the vicinities but deadly enemies of the Comanches, Tahuacanos, and Wacos." (Paraphrased from Lt. José María Sánchez y Tapia, *A Trip To Texas In 1828*)]

Berlandier wrote further of their first encounter with the Tancahueses and observations of hunger:

["They live in friendship with the Lipans and are at war with the Comanche and their allies. They rarely hunt buffalo for fear of a Comanche ambush. Therefore they live in the bleakness of poverty owing to their indolence, and many of them have died of hunger during the last few winters. In time of war they have been seen carrying the bleeding, severed limbs of the Tahuacanos they have slain as trophies of victory. Aside from that they can walk with extraordinary speed if need be, and they endure hunger better than any human beings I have ever known. When they are reduced to this extremity they can fasten belts around their waists and gradually draw them tighter until such time as they can find something to eat." (Paraphrased from Berlandier's *The Indians of Texas in 1830*)]

Since it was Berlandier's responsibility to learn all possible of the plants in Texas, and to make collections of them for Professor De Candolle, as well to study the native's uses of medicinal plants, Berlandier observed the following:

["The chief had us enter his cabin where he was seated by the fire employed in making a decoction of the leaves from a tree of the *Tetrandria monogynia* known in Texas as chocolate or *té del Indio*. (Berlandier referred to *Ilex vomitoria*, or *yaupon*, a shrub to make a ceremonial drink.) They use this decoction as a panacea for all scourges, while some several tribes such as the Texas, Caddos, and Carancahueses make it a daily drink. It is a powerful emmenagogne and an excellent stomachie. The Indians stew the leaves in water and use a bundle of small pieces of wood to make the decoction foam like chocolate. This extract is placed in another vessel or reduced a second time to a liquid state. It is their favorite drink." (Paraphrased from Berlandier's diary Vol. IV Chapter 2)

"Like the Caddo, they use the medicinal plant known as *Indian tea*, of which they are very fond. The Lipans, Comanches, and Tahuacanos never use it. I noted ground nuts with which they make a drink similar to orgeat (almond syrup). I also noted that they gathered roots of the genus *Nymphet* (water lilies) and after having been ground these produce a highly esteemed grayish flour with which they make a sort of cake." (Berlandier's *The Indians of Texas in 1830*)]

["The men go entirely naked save for a scrap of deer skin to cover their nudity in front and behind. Necklaces of beads and shells which they pick up in the streams are their only ornaments. The women wear a very short skirt tied to a point at each side, making a sort of curved apron in front and back. The most distinctive feature of the Tancahueses is their way of decorating their faces and bosoms. One, two, or three black lines are tattooed on their faces, beginning on the forehead and running down the nose to the chin. The breasts are painted with concentric circles centered on the nipples." (Paraphrased from Berlandier's *The Indians of Texas in 1830*)]

Chapter Nine
ENCOUNTER WITH THE FOLEYS

After departing the village of the Tancahueses and encampment on the Lavaca in order to repair a wagon wheel, the Boundary Commission *en route* to San Felipe on the Brazos had gone little farther the next day when another wheel on a wagon broke and "fell off in pieces" near the Navidad. The breakdown happened near to a pioneer homestead where a gentleman named Washington Green Lee Foley [later in life known casually as "Old Foley"] lived, farmed, and ranched. And while the wheel was under repair at the site of the break, Berlandier, Chowell, and Lt. Sánchez took opportunity to meet and query the family on matters of pioneer life for reports required of the Boundary Commission for needs of the Interior Ministry.

"Hello!" Berlandier called out, now seeing the gentleman of the house exit the door attracted by the commotion of their approach. It was a type of home common to pioneer era construction built with hand hewn logs, whip sawn boards, and froe split shingles. Across the entire front there stood a pillared roofed-over porch.

"Hello to you!" Foley called back, puzzled by their presence, And with him there was a very pretty girl about fourteen years of age with long dark curls and dark-brown eyes and who had the same aura of youthful innocence as that observed of the pretty Gonzales girl only a few days previously.

After a moment of cordial introductions among the men Berlandier turned to the, indeed, very pretty young girl and asked in an appealing if not alluring French-drenched accent: "And what is *your* name, *mademoiselle?*"

"Its Elizabeth Elmira!" she replied, shyly, though smiling within by the attention of the handsome young Frenchman and being referred to as a *mademoiselle*; then lowered her eyes to avoid a lingering eye contact.

[Elizabeth Elmira (Betsy) Foley was the "apple of her father's eye." (As said of her by Paul C. Boethel in *Ole Foley*)]

"Do you have a nickname?" Berlandier asked, curiously, but with the purpose to engage her further into a flirtatious conversation.

"Yes sir…its Betsy." She replied looking up demurely, then down again but then took the opportunity to break away from the conversation by turning back indoors and dutifully bringing out extra chairs for their guests to sit on the porch, just as the Gonzales girl had done so "charmingly gracious." With the men and Betsy seated, wife and mother, Sarah Foley, now joined the group with a pot of coffee fortuitously just brewed, and a platter of sugar cookies likewise just baked that morning by Betsy.

Berlandier wrote of a somewhat similar encounter and behavior:

> ["It was in Gonzales on the Guadalupe that we first perceived the character of the Anglo-Americans, that despite the fact we were reduced to seeking shade in under the trees, often around their houses, and though well received otherwise, there was not one of them who invited us inside." (Paraphrased from Berlandier's diary Vol. IV Chapter 2).

Of a similar incident on the Brazos some days later, Sánchez wrote:

> ["They carried on a conversation with us but did not offer us entry into the house." (José María Sánchez y Tapia, "A Trip To Texas In 1828.")]

"And what is the name of your friend there?" Berlandier asked to further his conversation with the pretty girl in reference to the large red wolf, a species common to the area that ambled over to sit beside Betsy, obviously quite friendly by the wags of its tail.

"Growler" she replied as she patted and scratched up and down his back and pulled affectionately on his big ears. Betsy offered other information that he got his name because he growled about things but didn't bark like dogs will do.

"He sometimes howls loudly when responding to others off in the distance somewhere but he never joins them," Betsy explained.

To that, Berlandier agreed with his knowledge of the nature of wolves often heard loudly at night.

"We found him as a pup in a den in the river bank half starved after being abandoned for some reason. We heard him whimpering down deep inside and I crawled in to pull him out. But we, mostly me, nursed him back to good health and ever since Growler has followed me wherever I go."

["In captivity wolves often grow up docile and will treat human friends as pack mates." (Allen)]

"That seems to be the nature of wolves...to tame easily. Wolves of one kind or another are common in Indian villages, especially like yours when raised as pups...and he obviously chose you as the 'alpha' of his pack." Berlandier grinned.

"What does that mean?"

"That you are the number one in his life, so to speak. You fed him when little and raised him for which he owes you his loyalty and affection."

"Growler has been a good pet for Betsy," Foley piped in to say, "He has given her...us...no problem. But the wild ones around here often give us troubles with the livestock."

But to address another subject important for his reports to the Ministry—though he was sure already of the reply—Berlandier turned to Foley and asked: "Have Indians been any problems around here?"

"As everywhere!" he retorted, wondering why the question even needed to be asked. "The Tancahueses and Lipans are a bit okay... friendly enough when it behooves them...but the Comanches and Tahuacanos raid all across the land when down this way hunting buffalo. And whenever here we have problems with the devils stealing our cattle and horses. We lose one or two now and then." But then with a chuckle, and the others in like response, remarked: "And we get one or two of them...now and then."

Washington Green Lee Foley [as described of him by biographer Paul C. Boethel] was an "odd one" in his demeanor; frugal, tight with his money, and "quaint" in his dress; the words "gruff, eccentric and foul-mouthed" also described him well. He could break out laughing after a pint of home brew and roar heartily when hearing good knee-slapping stories. And if another pint so moved him he had a good number of his own to tell though most weren't meant for mixed company or tender ears.

But what the crusty, cantankerous, often profane "odd one" lacked in social graces and literary ability, he understood money, land, and controversies. As a patriot to the causes, Foley stood firmly sympathetic to the political aspirations of a budding new State of Texas to separate from Mexico even if by revolution.

On questioning by his guests of the day, Foley told of the family's settlement and concerns on the frontier after emigrating from Alabama.

"We put up a sign of 'Gone to Texas' on the door of our cabin when we left Alabama with all of the belongings that we could carry in two covered wagons pulled by teams of oxen, moved here to the frontier. It was a long hard hazardous journey west to the Mississippi and down on a ferry to New Orleans and then overland across the Sabine, Trinity, to San Felipe on the Brazos, and finally across the Colorado to settle here as members in these parts of the Hallett settlement.

"That's hard to imagine that you got this far with all of the many rivers and the bigger ones at that," Berlandier remarked with nods of agreement from Chowell and Sánchez. "*We* were able…rather easily I should mention when coming up from Mexico…to ford the Rio Bravo at Laredo. It was quite wide but fortunately shallow…only about waist deep…and people there commonly wade it back and forth. Beyond Béxar, the creeks and streams were shallow and though the Guadalupe was deep it was easy to cross with kindly help of the Gonzales people by use of a flatboat for a ferry. Our horses just swam across."

"What made you want to come so far from Alabama?" Chowell asked, curiously. Sánchez piped up in support of the question that "Surely you must have known in advance about Texas as a land of wild animals and hostile Indians. And you surely knew ahead of time that some families return home after only about the second or third Indian raid to burn them out."

"Well, we had heard all of that." Foley said with a chuckle. "But our *want* for coming here as you asked was the offers of free land to be one of the three hundred American families that empresario Stephen F. Austin needed to gain title to his land-grant colony. The *doing* of the wanting was…well…just being daring enough." Foley remarked with a wry grin.

"You mean 'just being dumb enough!'" Sarah interjected, though said with a smile and a pat on Foley's arm.

"That, too," Foley replied with a chuckle. "But there *are* the dangers" he added, sorrowfully. "Our son Tucker was killed by marauding Indians not long ago and the heathens recently killed old man Lyons on the Navidad just south of here a few miles down in the Sweet Home community. They abducted his young son who has not yet been found one way or another and the same Indians that may have been Tawakonis, played hell later with the Douglass and O'Dougherty families just south of here below the Hallett area. We knew them all."

"What happened?" Berlandier asked, needing to know all that he could learn concerning Indian depredations for his reports on such matters back to the Ministry.

"Could we talk about something else?" Sarah whispered aside to Foley, quietly. "Betsy knew the poor girls."

"Well, Sarah," Foley replied rather bluntly, "Betsy knows already of what happened to the three girls and it won't harm her no more to be reminded of the dangers when Indians are lurking about, even if seemingly friendly." Sarah gave a hesitant though now a reluctant nod of agreement, and with a sympathetic look to Betsy for what she was about to hear again.

"Well then." Foley continued to the men. "As I was starting to say, O'Dougherty was a widower with two very pretty daughters aged twelve and fourteen, and Douglass had a wife with a fourteen year old daughter. Both had a son, and at the time of a raid on the two neighboring homes the two boys happened to be away together, but the one mother and three girls were visiting. On return, the boys found their fathers dead at their cabins shot with arrows and scalped and unmanned in the most obscene of ways. At first they thought that the mother and three girls had been abducted and carried away as they weren't around anywhere close and it wasn't until the next morning that searchers found all four of them dead in an oak motte about a mile away where they had been taken and___"

"Just hush!" Sarah interjected to interrupt the story. "There is no need to say anything more. I think the men must know what happened to them, and Betsy doesn't need to hear again the gory details of how they were found."

"Well, the men need to know that when found," the irreverent "Ole Foley" who minces no words in telling something like it was, "they were found stripped of their clothing and mutilated beyond almost all recognition even as to their gender, what with those parts of them needed to know were taken for God-damned trophies, and all of the hair on their heads was likewise taken except for some strands of it still attached to skull fragments."

"That's horrifying to hear and especially of them being your daughter's friends," Sánchez remarked to Foley with a look of sympathy to young Betsy, "but we already know of such things happening. If you don't know of it already two girls were recently abducted up near York Creek. We just heard the news when in Gonzales."

"Good Lord, at York Creek too. We didn't know!" Sarah exclaimed.

"No, we hadn't heard," Foley spoke up, "but it was likely those damned same Tawakonis who have been reported recently up along the Guadalupe. What happened?"

"All *we* know is that late one afternoon two ten and twelve year-old sisters were out penning up livestock for the night and the mother heard them to start screaming. She ran out to help though not knowing at first the problems but then saw five Indians on horses ride off with them. By the time the mother and neighbors could form a posse it was already dark and the two girls were long gone and nothing of them one way or another has yet been found."

"Will they ever be?" Betsy asked, hopefully.

"Probably not as few girls carried off like those two were are ever found or heard of again and if still alive they are likely already suffering a fate worse than death itself off in a God-forsaken camp somewhere and likely one far away. The grieving mother still has hopes of finding her daughters but hope is all that keeps her going."

"Oh heaven!" Sarah exclaimed in response to the story of a mother's grief. Could such for a daughter ever be hers?

"We're always watchful for such things happening around here," Foley commented.

"Watchful of Betsy especially!" Sarah interjected with weak exchanges of smiles between the mother and daughter.

"Betsy knows never to wander off anywhere alone" the father added, "and we take refuge out back in the stockade if we see or have reasons to think that Indians are close about."

["A reliable sign of the approach of Indians in the early days was the antics of milk cows that gave evidence of fright when scenting them." (Paul C. Boethel). "Our horses looked in the direction of the Indians and began to sniff and snort and move about uneasily." (J.H. Jenkins). "Wild bulls, cows, horses, donkeys, and deer, bears, coyotes, and wolves, all flee at the approach of Indians when seen or scented." (José María Sánchez y Tapia). "Spanish horses could smell Karankawas as far as five miles away, and their odor caused horses and cattle to run away from them." (Noah Smithwick).]

"Even if the devils should ever set fire to our cabin…always a danger in these areas with log-built houses…but our adobe stockade can't be burned, and in where we will be well armed for a defense. Sarah and Betsy are both good shots, Betsy especially."

At the comment Berlandier and Betsy exchanged looks and smiles but Betsy quickly lowered her eyes again to avoid a lingering eye contact.

"With the Indians often hostile and dangerous as they are," Foley added to his story, "we here in these regions travel well armed wherever we go."

["People travel with a good lookout for a person is never safe in the Indian ranges." (William Bollaert, Ethnologist). "Men and women often rode long distances for a dance in honor of a new bride but such festivities often came to sudden halts when Indian raids caused the men to drop the hands of their dancing partners and seize their rifles." (Betty J. Mills, Historian). Historian Paul Boethel wrote of the Lavaca and Navidad River areas "being hit hard by marauding Indians."

Historian Mary C. Bond wrote of the Washington Foley family "being hit hard by them often." Elizabeth Elmira's older brother, Tucker, was killed by Comanches in a murderous chase, although a traveling companion managed to escape (Boethel, Smithwick, and Wilbarger).]

"We do," Sarah spoke up to add, "especially at night if we get suspicious when hearing owl hoots and wolf howls or during the day quail or turkey calls. Such are commonly heard around here anyway but it's common knowledge that Indians use them for signals."

"Yeah!" Betsy piped in. "Lucky for us, Growler seems to know the differences. He pricks his ears to all, but growls only to Indian sounds. And when he does, and if we also hear chirping crickets or croaking frogs outside suddenly going silent in the night we snuff out the candles to be safer."

"Good idea!" Berlandier said in agreement with the comments, and a smile to Betsy who grinned in return as she patted Growler atop his head as an additional affectionate sign of appreciation.

To change the topic of conversation, Sánchez had need of information for the Interior Ministry on the sentiments among Anglo pioneers towards the government. He, personally, was disgruntled with North Americans in *Coahuila y Tejas* and what seemed to him with airs of arrogance.

So here it was with such feelings that Lieutenant José María Sánchez y Tapia sat before Washington Green Lee Foley, an Anglo-American thought by Sánchez as being one of the too many already taking over the land.

"The overwhelming sentiments," Foley replied to the question, "are to keep Mexico beholden to its 1824 State's Rights provisions allowing Texas to become its own State apart from Coahuila when sufficiently populated and supported, and to have closer ties to the United States." Such said was not what Sánchez wanted to hear although he fully expected such an answer.

"But, Mr. Foley," Sánchez retorted, "there are rumors long circulating around Béxar that North Americans from Gonzales all the way eastward to Nacogdoches and San Augustine are thinking of breaking from Mexico completely…to become a Republic or petition the United States for statehood."

"To that, I can only say that for all intents and purposes we here in the colonies consider ourselves American, having come from there and more loyal to the United States than to Mexico. That in large part is because the United States all across the west maintains regional forts to protect its citizens, while down here we never see a soldier of any stripe for protection against Indians, and until today you are only the first military person I've seen, or anyone else so far as I know." [Foley left unsaid, however, that Stephen F. Austin was already forming a volunteer Texas militia in case of an armed conflict with Mexico, and to help defend colonists against Indian raids.]

Sánchez liked even less of what he was hearing but remained silent although he stood to stretch his legs for a moment and for longer moments to lean against a porch post gazing off into the distance, lost momentarily in his thoughts. Sánchez was born in Monterrey and was proudly Mexican. His patriotism to his native land was firmly planted in the revolutionary period of Mexico's own 1810 to 1821 rebellion against Spain. While he himself was a revolutionist just in the past decade, he was angered by Foley's support of rumblings for Texas independence and that American settlers, all the more arrogant in his opinion, seemed little interested or obligated to live up to settlement agreements in exchange for free lands.

Few of the pioneer settlers had learned to speak Spanish as required by law since Spanish was the legal language of the land, and all laws were written in it. But few Americans understood the language *or* the laws, or could even read them. Moreover, few of other faiths had converted to Catholicism also required by law, although Sánchez had to admit to his self that the reason was largely due to the fact that there were no Catholic churches anywhere in the colonies east of Béxar.

He did therefore have to give Americans some measure of credit for the inopportunity of conversion but with that aside, immigration laws also required that all settlers of any faith had to be of "good moral character" in order to be granted citizenship. But there were no means to ensure such a restriction or were there any extradition laws to return an immigrant from another State for any reason.

61

Moreover, the flood of immigrants into Texas, legal or not, now outnumbered nationals by twenty to one and Sánchez could already sense what Foley had just said, that Texas already considers itself as American and would likely petition for Statehood. But, then, that would assuredly brew a revolution as Mexico wouldn't willingly grant such a petition, and Foley had just remarked that no one in his part of the colonies ever sees a Mexican soldier. So who is to oppose them?

Sánchez had to wonder about how Mexico could defend itself against a revolution by Texans already numbering in the thousands *unless* Mexico brought in massive numbers of troops, cavalry, and artillery from as far as Mexico City to counter a revolution. And he had observed already that the several hundred presidio troops presently in Laredo and Béxar have difficulties even to defend Texas against small bands of only fifty or so marauding Indians bent on just murder and plunder.

Moreover, the Boundary Commission of which he was a participant had just spent two difficult months getting from Mexico City to the Rio Bravo at only about eight miles a day on average over roads hard to follow and so rocky and rough most of the way that the wagons kept breaking down from broken wheels and axles. Sánchez himself was a military man and knew the almost unimaginable if not nearly impossible logistics of such an operation to transport the heavy artillery pieces that would be needed plus many dozens of horse drawn supply wagons for a thousand or more troops and in the northerly desert regions there were shortages of water and forage for the many hundreds of horses needed.

Sánchez who already considered Anglo-Americans arrogant, now thought more so of them to likely force Mexico to such extremes when they had willingly accepted sovereign Mexican law when agreeing to Mexican citizenship. They owed it to Mexico to keep Texas Mexican and to remain Mexican citizens, but obviously had little intentions to do so. Such arrogance!

Sánchez did however stand sympathetic to the plights of Americans with the hostile indigenes that murdered, scalped, and abducted girls and young women of breeding age for unthinkable purposes. They were the same kinds of problems far south into Mexico long experienced already from marauding Comanches and Lipan Apaches raiding haciendas and ranchos and stealing the animals, abducting the girls, and killing all others. And just today he learned of the tragedy of the three friends of Betsy's, and how easy it could have been that pretty Betsy would have been one of them.

Still more, he knew from reliable sources within the ranks that in case of a revolution Mexico would solicit the chiefs of amenable tribes as allies to fight the Texans, to "set flames to the frontier and to fill the air with screams of Texan women and children." With such thoughts in mind while gazing off into the distance, Sánchez could not help but to turn and look back at Sarah and Betsy Foley, a lovely lady and such a pretty girl. Such things that could happen to either or both of them was unimaginable even to think about, and for the sakes of humanity Sánchez couldn't wish those kinds of horrors on anyone, not even North Americans.

Sánchez turned back, too, to question Foley more of local problems with Indians and needs. The Interior Ministry wanted to know, and Berlandier himself was asked to determine extents of Indian problems on the frontier and the dispositions and hostilities of them.

"Around here we're in need of a well armed militia to help us fight the God-damned Comanche and Tahuacano devils," profane Foley stated with emphasis.

"Shssh!" Sarah cautioned her husband of such language in front of Betsy.

"Well if the Lieutenant is here to ask questions I feel need to give him the answers that he may, or may not want to hear. And what I hear about the presidio soldiers down in Laredo and Béxar is that the villagers down there live close to the presidios for protection from Indians and travel little more than a mile away in any direction for the fears of those lurking around and waiting on ambush opportunities, but even at that get blessed little of any military help.

"Around here, there isn't even a pretense for help. Families in these parts have to gather neighbors, often from miles around to form their own posses. But the Indians practice hit and run skirmishes and by the time that a large enough posse can be formed to take on a band up to fifty or more hostiles the culprits are long gone. And even for it to happen once be one too many when the damnable heathens carry off one of our girls or kill them for trophy parts."

"We understand your concerns Mr. and Mrs. Foley." Sánchez spoke up to say. "There are Indian raids south of here all the way down to Monterrey, Saltillo, as well as around Chihuahua filling up our cemeteries down there with murdered men, women, and children. They even raid the missions and kill the priests. They have no concepts of Christian moralities."

"Well I'm glad to hear such an admission to your own problems," Foley said, "and that far south as you say. We up here have long believed that the main reason eight years ago Mexico opened its Sabine border for immigrants from the States was so that increasing numbers of Americans would take the brunt of raids and pressure off your own people, especially from the Comanches."

"Well" Berlandier interjected to say, feeling *some* need for clarification of the problems. "They *are* by the inherent nature of them compared to Christian standards, unholy, uncivilized, undependable, and untrustworthy."

"Those are no secrets around here," Foley said, and to stress his own uses of "*un*" words stated that "Just a year ago the unholy devils as you speak of them were so **un**friendly that they '**un**manned' the Gonzales area for two years by driving survivors to Columbus and San Felipe for protection…if those are other of any '*un*' words you may want to use." Foley stresses the "uns."

"And the worst for us personally is that our son Tucker…Betsy's brother…was tortured and killed by the devils close to Gonzales. They sliced off the soles of his feet and made him walk that way…obviously just for the amusement of hearing his cries from the pains…and then the devils thrust him through with spears and scalped and unmanned him too. That's how we found and buried him.

"And how more '*unned*' can the damnable heathens be than to have mutilated the poor girls just south of here down in Sweet Home by scalping them all over and by slicing off their___"

"Darn it!" Sarah interrupted Foley again. "Just hush! It's not what Betsy needs to hear any more of."

"Well…my apology," he grumbled. "But our guests here from other parts need to know that around here the devils are considered *un*worthy for any consideration of the brotherhood of man…if Mr. Berlandier here needs still another '*un*' word for his list."

"Our deepest sympathies to the loss of your son, Mr. Foley and Mrs. Foley, and the manner of it...and to Betsy for what happened to her brother and friends." Sánchez expressed the sincerest of his sorrow to the family while looking again at pretty Betsy who now reminded him all the more of the young girl in Gonzales, and all the more his fearful concerns for both girls when "smiles could someday turn to tears."

"Well," Berlandier spoke up again to say more of the Comanches though not to praise them. "They are not all of one tribe but are of at least ten bands widely scattered and headed by different chiefs. Each band small or large...some up to several hundred...is loyal only to its own, and the one of several hundred presently roaming the Béxar area is friendly enough in order to trade buffalo skins for coveted village goods...especially mirrors and tweezers for their vanity as well as trinkets and calico cloths for the women. A mirror alone is worth a bundle of buffalo hides. But, obviously, the band around here is *un*friendly," Berlandier said with another emphasis in the use of another "un" word.

The emphasis however drew a chuckle from Foley and the others, though cantankerous Ole Foley frowned while expressing his embittered opinions on the needs of military help to fight Indians.

"And more priests," Sarah spoke up to add to the needs.

"What in God's name for?" Foley snapped back.

"To take care of marriages around here!" Sarah retorted.

"Damn it! Sarah___"

"Shssh!" she cautioned again of his language.

"Well we don't need any of them so-called Brown Robed mackerel-snatchers for marriages, and I *will* be damned if we have to turn ourselves into Catholics just to get Betsy married someday, what with all that pagan mumbo-jumbo stuff of theirs in a language that even the Romans no longer speak. And what's with all the gesticulations, genuflects, burned incense with smoke, and the holy signs of the cross? What's with the need for holy water to dip in? The Navidad water around here is holy enough just from the name of it and we even bathe in it which is a hell of lot more water used than when the devoted only get sprinkled with it.

"Well, a Bah Humbug to it all!" Foley grumbled. "When the time comes we'll just take Betsy back to Alabama for something more

Christian in a marriage." Berlandier, Chowell and Sánchez, Roman Catholics, glanced at one another and frowned a bit.

[Anglo-American colonists in Mexico were required by law to convert to Catholicism in order to settle in Texas although few did and marriages could be performed only by a priest though there were no Catholic churches east of Béxar. Early in the colonies there was only one priest, a Father Michael Muldoon who *did* live in San Felipe but in his absence marriages elsewhere *could* be performed by agreement with a mayor of a settlement or a judge and by payment of a bond guaranteeing that a couple would be officially married on the next rounds of a priest in the name of the church. But forfeit of the required bond was the only action needed for an annulment if the marriage failed before the next round of the priest that could be weeks.]

[History doesn't record in what Protestant faith that Elizabeth Elmira (Betsy) Foley (1814-1875) was married to John Samuel Woods (1795-1864) but the two were wed on September 4, 1831, when Betsy would have been seventeen, just three years after the 1828 time frame of this story. But Historian Paul C. Boethel *does* place their marriage in Rodgersville, Alabama, and eventual settlement on the Lavaca River in a location still known as "Woods' Place" or "Woods' Crossing" just west a few miles of the Foley homestead.

Betsy Woods died at the age of 62, and aside from personal wealth her property consisted of 13,087 acres of land with an additional 4,381 acres listed in the names of her heirs.

In a genealogy of the Woods family, Willie F. Woods III, names twelve children of the Woods/Foley union from 1832 to 1856; one of whom, Sarah Louise (Louisa) Woods, is the heroine in the story *Louisa of Woods' Crossing*.]

Lt. Sánchez of the Mexican military and a patriot to his country restrained expressions of his innermost feelings to the Foleys but wrote the following report to the Ministry, paraphrased:

["The Americans from the north are taking possession of the lands that best suit them to build their homes and raise their families and crops, and without any permission as no one is here to prevent them, not even the military if such action is necessary.

"Thus, the majority of inhabitants in the easternmost regions of Texas are from America and the government of Coahuila y Tejas with its seat far to the south in Saltillo is in need of further measures to further prevent this precious part of the land from being stolen by foreign hands."

Critical of his own government in Mexico, Sánchez further wrote: "Thus the vigilance of our highest authorities has been lax while our enemies do not lose a single opportunity of advancing towards their treacherous design to take over this land."]

Thus, there occurred the encounter with the Foley family and the learning of their homestead location, lifestyles, beliefs, and sentiments, and as Sánchez wrote: "North Americans were choosing lands that suited them the best."

Foley liked the Navidad area to *his* liking which, indeed, "suited him best." It was a pretty country sufficiently timbered and well-suited for corn, cotton and stock. Perch, trout, and catfish swam the river while buffalos, deer, bears, peccaries, turkeys, and prairie hens roamed the range. Ducks and geese were abundant as well as squirrels, hares and rabbits. Fruit and nut trees grew abundantly in the forests—pecans and walnuts were harvested by the cartloads—and everywhere wild grapes grew for jams, jellies, and wines. Some vines grew to the sunny tops of the tallest trees.

Water and foodstuffs, and timber for housing, sheds and pens, and soil for planting supplied all the basics for survival on the frontier. The land was vacant and for the taking, and in his time "Ole Foley" farmed one of the largest cotton plantations in the State of Texas to became one of the richest men in the country.

It was believed if not true as Sánchez opined, that North Americans were "stealing the land."

Notes: The dialogue in this Chapter is necessarily fictionalized as in others though the topics of conversations are in keeping with the pioneer history of 1820s Texas derived from *Recollections of Early Texas by* John Holland Jenkins; the 1828 diaries of Jean Louis Berlandier and Lieutenant José María Sánchez as well as this Chapter in particular from Paul C. Boethel's 1981 treatise, *Ole Foley.)*

Chapter Ten

SAN FELIPE DE AUSTIN
AND CALAMITY

It had taken a full day's sojourn for the men to repair the wheel at an unnamed *paraje* (place) though to be called by them *El Campo de la Rueda* (the camp of the wheel) and where mosquitoes became worrisome enough in their travels to bother them considerably as did horseflies and bothersome gnats. The advance guard saw a black bear; startled coveys of quail; scared up turkeys; and through the evening and night heard the forest "reverberate with the yips of coyotes and the mournful howls of wolves." And with it all were the hums of mosquitoes and the incessant croaks of frogs and cricket chirps interspersed with occasional owl hoots.

It was all along the course of the entire journey that Berlandier made plant collections for his herbals (papered specimens) and observations of the larger flora. He took notes of such things as cacti common in the south from Laredo up through Béxar [including a species later named as *Echinocereus berlandieri* and now known popularly as "Berlandier's hedgehog cactus"]. Of the prickly pear cacti found largely in the south, Berlandier observed that "as one advances farther to the north, its diminution is very striking."

Berlandier wrote with interest of a seemingly optical illusion that after walking across plains but when entering trees "the forests made it seem as if going downhill as the unseen horizon appeared to lie below the level of the ground which we were tramping."

It was at the Guadalupe that the men first became bothered, considerably, with poison ivy. Berlandier took note of its prevalence especially in oaks, and wrote, paraphrased:

["The flowers and leaves have malefic properties. For instance, it causes those who approach it to swell in the body, and when the plant is flowering one often needs to

69

do no more than lie down nearby, not even touch it in order to be affected. When its effects have been felt, vinegar rubs sometime serve as an antidote against the swelling, but some soldiers of the escort swelled up considerably. Yet, some persons without taking any precautions will never feel its effect. I myself have rubbed the leaves and the flowers between my hands, have cut a host of specimens of it, and without knowing why have never been attacked."]

The Boundary Commission moved eastward ever so slowly in direction of the Sabine borderlands of *Coahuila y Tejas* with the Territory of Louisiana in the areas of Nacogdoches and San Augustine. Whenever going through forests surrounding the meadows it was often necessary to cut down trees in order to widen the route for their wagons, especially for the General's oversized carriage. The recently surveyed road that connected Gonzales with San Felipe was little improved, little traveled, and yet little lived along, and so it happened one day as the entourage neared the Colorado that "their eyes were gladdened by the sight of a dwelling surrounded by fields and herds."

Messrs. Berlandier, Chowell, and Lieutenant Sánchez made contact with the owner, a Mr. William B. DeWees who revealed on questioning that he had received title to the land in 1824 and spent his only money at the time, two hundred pesos, to buy seed stock for his now large herds of pigs, cattle, and some horses. On inquiry about Indian troubles, Mr. DeWees told of being taken into captivity by Huecos [Wacos] when *en route* from Missouri together with some inhabitants from Béxar. But "the latter," he said, "knowledgable in the customs of the indigenes, knew how to obtain their liberty." Mr. DeWees told of other colonists along the river who early-on were attacked by Indians "but now are in peace."

Again as everywhere along the way, Berlandier collected plants and some animals and insects and made the following observation:

["When twilight fell I noticed the prairies come aglow with phosphorescent insects that shone all night. I recognized them as fireflies remarkable for the two yellow rings on their abdomen from which the scintillations emanate."]

Differing from what Lt. Sánchez and party had experienced by North Americans on the Guadalupe and the Navidad, their reception by Mr. DeWees on the Colorado was much improved. Sánchez wrote of "being given excellent lodging and the meals being very good."

Yet three days later on arrival in San Felipe on the Brazos, Sánchez reported observations further supporting poor feelings for North Americans. Sánchez wrote:

["This village settled by Mr. Stephen Austin, a native of the United States of the North, consists of forty or fifty wooden houses on the western bank of the *Rio de los Brazos de Dios* but lie in an irregular and desultory manner. Its population is nearly two hundred persons of which only ten are Mexican, for the balance are all Americans from the North with an occasional European. Two wretched little stores supply the inhabitants; one sells only whiskey, rum, sugar, and coffee; the other rice, flour, lard, and cheap cloth.

"The inhabitants in general in my opinion are lazy people not of good character. Some of them cultivate their small farms but this task they usually entrust to their Negro slaves whom they treat with considerable harshness. Beyond the village in an immense stretch of land are scattered families brought by Stephen Austin which today number more than two thousand persons.

"The policy of this empresario, evident in all his actions have, as one may say, lulled the authorities into a sense of security while he works diligently for his own ends. In my judgment, the spark that will someday start the conflagration to deprive us of Texas will originate from this colony and because the government does not take vigorous measures to prevent it. Perhaps it does not realize the value of what it is about to lose."]

Lieutenant Sánchez wrote more of one particular person in San Felipe, a Mr. Groce who history records as a staunch patriot to Texas in conflicts with the Mexicans by supplying the army with corn, beef, horses and mules. As a wealthy plantation owner Groce raised cotton; brought the first gin to Texas; and received recognitions for selling the first twenty-five bales.

Yet, despite the above known of Mr. Groce the following reflects Sánchez's disgruntled, derogatory opinion(s) of North Americans in general.

["Mr. Groce came from the United States to establish himself on the eastern side of the river and brought with him 116 slaves of both sexes of which most were stolen. Likewise he has a great many head of cattle, innumerable hogs, and a great number of horses, but he is a man who does not enjoy his wealth because he is extremely stingy, and he treats his slaves with great cruelty." (Paraphrased from Sánchez, *A Trip to Texas in1828*)]

Rafael Chowell also uttered unflattering remarks of Mr. Groce, and of the three diarists including Berlandier studying the land and in writing of the people, Sánchez and Chowell were the most critical in observations and opinions of Americans. But Berlandier being a liberally educated Frenchman wrote more disparagingly of the Mexican people:

["There exists among the Mexican people a considerable number presenting a quite disgusting picture producing a very disagreeable effect on me. Murders are so common among the rabble that foreigners would be horrified if it were possible to procure exact statistics for this crime. Throughout the interior of Mexico bands of thieves along roads and in villages affect and disquiet peaceable citizens." (Paraphrased from Berlandier's diary Vol. II Chapter 2.)]

["The Mexicans in Texas were perceived different from and somewhat inferior to Anglo citizens of the rest of the State. They (the Mexicans) were irresponsible, lazy, and backward. The three diarists (Berlandier, Sánchez, and Terán) expected to find the frontier a primitive, slothful, degenerate, and violent place, and their expectations obviously colored what they actually saw and wrote." (Paraphrased from the Introduction to *Texas by Terán* by John Wheat)]

Though employed primarily as a botanist and a naturalist, Berlandier helped gather intelligence for the Boundary Commission on political situations, wealth, and the sentiments of the populace in order to make recommendations to the Interior Ministry for ways to close the boundaries between Texas and the United States [that did happen in 1830 and with a ban on any further importation of slaves].

The above negative feelings of Mr. Groce were tempered however by experiences of the Commission party some days later when Berlandier became sick and received medical attention by the Groce family. But so it happened for the next several days that Berlandier continued with his fever [malaria], then also that of the General becoming so serious that for a night the General's death seemed possible.

Lt. Sanchez wrote (paraphrased):

["In the morning of May 16 Mr. Berlandier and others in our party including the General began feeling ill and in the afternoon we stopped at the house of a North American named Nolan who provided us with milk and chickens to feed them. Our patients continued to grow worse and it was decided to make a bed in the carriage for Mr. Berlandier along with the General and, under it, a hammock for the cook, John. Mr. Chowel took charge of the sick and Mr. Batres and I took charge of the kitchen about which Mr. Batres and I understood not a thing.

"In the afternoon the General became more ill and he would have been as ill as Mr. Berlandier had not an occurrence saved him. The General had perspired so freely through the night that on the following day he felt much better.

"May 19-20. We stayed in the same place and the sicker men continued to grow worse, their condition being serious except that of Salomé who became better. By the 27th the sick men seemed to have improved after being doctored by Mr. Chowell but an additional four others also fell ill with the same fever for this place is very sickly. The swarms of mosquitoes in these swampy lands and lack of adequate food added greatly to this calamity. Mr. Batres is also now sick from the mosquito bites. May the Lord have pity on us all?

"By May 29 the General now well decided that Mr. Chowell, Mr. Berlandier and Colonel Batres should return to Béxar with the instrument and a supply wagon, and even the General's carriage still for a bed for Berlandier. And that the General and I should continue to Nacogdoches taking only the baggage most needed in another wagon and seven men as an escort. All others were to return. It must have been about two in the afternoon when we sadly took leave of the others of our travelling companions preparing to return to Béxar." (Jose María Sánchez; *A Trip to Texas in 1828*).]

The diary of General Manuel de Mier y Terán collaborates that above written by Sánchez, and on May 26 wrote: "We are all [additionally] sick from emaciation and from insect bites which have ulcerated. The healthiest ones of us are Sánchez and Chowell" [implying that Berlandier was the sickest].

On May 29 the General verified that written by Sánchez about continuing on to Nacogdoches:

["I am being accompanied by Lieutenant Sánchez while the rest are returning to Béxar." (*Texas by Terán, On His 1828 Inspection of Texas*)]

Notes: The following is paraphrased from John C. Ewers, Editor of Berlandier's *The Indians of Texas in 1830*.

["Bad luck began to plague Terán's party when he and his men were in San Felipe de Austin. Heavy spring rains so swelled the Brazos that it became impossible to cross, making it necessary for them to wait impatiently for the water to subside. By the 9th a crossing was at last possible by use of a ferry to continue on to Nacogdoches but by May 17 Berlandier was very sick with fever, as were others, by the time the party reached the Trinity River. There, the General decided to divide his command to send the sicker ones back to San Antonio."]

Chapter Eleven
BACK TO BÉXAR

When Berlandier and the others of the Boundary Commission under command of General Terán left San Antonio de Béxar of the thirteenth of April, 1828, the intention of the entire party was to go to Nacogdoches and from there along the banks of the Sabine River borderline between Coahuila y Tejas and Louisiana. Part of the reason was to scout out the land for the feasibility of closing the border between Mexico and the United States to stop any and all future immigration from North America. But also to study the several Indian tribes there and to investigate the willingness and practicality of having tribes side with Mexico in case of a revolution with Texans that did happen eight years later in 1836. It was then if so persuaded that the Cherokees alone with several thousand members in their tribe *could* play a major role. [But such never happened for any Indian tribe to cooperate.]

By the time of reaching the Trinity, the usual rainy season had already started but some storms had especially torrential rains and high winds. The rivers and creeks flooded extraordinarily. The inundation of large parts of the route were turning already poor roads into muddy quagmires and the swarms of mosquitoes, and the fear of losing all of the harness mules by horseflies biting and bleeding them remorselessly, obliged the General to divide the party into two groups and necessarily to take different routes.

One group composed of General Terán and Lieutenant Sánchez and part of the dragoon escorts followed the intended route on to Nacogdoches, whereas Lt. Colonel Batres, Señor Chowell and Monsieur Berlandier returned to Béxar with most of the baggage, the instrument wagon with collecting materials and Berlandier's plant collections, and even the General's carriage returned, still to be used as a bed for Berlandier the sickest of them all. Moreover and importantly for safety in the Indian territories, the others in Berlandier's group were the remainder of the dragoon escort.

To shorten the route and to avoid the inundations of lower Texas, Berlandier's group travelled what was known in its day as the Camino de Arriba [Upper Road] where there were fewer marshes; streams easier to cross; but less fortunate and less safe the route was most exposed to attacks by hostile Indians, especially by the Comanches, Wacos and the Tawakoni allies often present there. Also along that route, only a single dwelling was known and that being on the banks of the Brazos River. However, the contingent of armed dragoons likely dissuaded and prevented any Indian attacks.

Berlandier wrote in his diary (paraphrased):

["We left without being able beforehand to procure more provisions for ourselves but were soon fortunate to be joined by two Kickapoo Indians who performed the role of hunters and every day brought us some white-tailed deer which they killed. With certain instruments which they make themselves, they imitate the voice of the wild animals they wish to obtain and attract them to where they hide, and then when the animals are enticed close enough, they kill them.

"We spent our first night on the banks of a small arroyo with a shallow flow. The countryside mostly was composed of a succession of hills broken by small forests, and prairies strewn with flowers in such profusion that they covered the entire surface of the ground." (Volume IV Chapter 3)]

Similarly of the same kinds of vistas when en route to Nacogdoches, José Sánchez wrote:

["The countryside is bedecked with many wildflowers, and when one inhales the perfume of them the soul seems to revel in joy." (*A Trip to Texas in 1828*)]

On June 2, Berlandier saw evidences of what may have been the first recorded tornado or a devastating downdraft in the early pioneer era of Texas.

["At the Arroyo de Los Tinajeros [Stream of the Potholes] and on the edge of a large forest not far away we found a ranchera of indigenes which was abandoned. As soon as we entered the wood we saw the traces of a storm which had probably blown in January or February. The tops of all of the oak trees were broken and lay scattered on the ground. A very small number of these ancient and robust trees had resisted the wind, and some stands whose trunks had a diameter of one and a half to two feet had been broken and looked as if they had been broken off close to their base. The ground all about was strewn with broken branches, witnesses of the force of the storm. Though most of the trees were very badly damaged they seemed to be still growing.

"Beyond, a small prairie not far from that disastrous scene one finds the edge of a forest which shades the banks of the Brazos River. It is on the northern bank a little below the place where the river is joined by the branch from the northwest called Brazo Chico [Little Arm] that one finds a dwelling of Americans. The host is an unfortunate old man but hospitable and obliging, and who is a Creole from the United States of America. He lives there with his children and who is continually harassed by the Wacos and Tawakonis who come there to steal his horses, cows and food crops. The river like all of those in Texas that had risen considerably that year had carried off from the unfortunate colonist an entire house situated on the riverside, and had destroyed his fields of corn on the other bank. Despite his misery he lived the greatest of cheerfulness and content with his lot when a traveler came to him to rest.

"We sojourned there until the eighth of June, camping close to the colonist's hut but where all were persecuted by the insects [likely mosquitoes, gadflies and gnats]. As we were devoid of aid for the rest of the route, Lt. Colonel Batres sent two soldiers to Béxar to seek additional medications and food. For a long time we had lacked biscuits and salt and were reduced to living off the hunting of the two Kickapoos and to corn bread which we never encountered except in the dwellings. It resembled sandstone more than a food but made with corn that had been reduced to very course flour in hand mills, thereafter only the barely cracked grains are separated with a large sieve full of holes.

"During the long sojourn there while awaiting the needed medications we spent time to open a road in the forest on the other bank, for the road that once existed there had been destroyed by flooding of the river." (Paraphrased from Volume IV Chapter 3)]

The lengthy sojourn and serendipitous good luck to observe and mingle with several members from various Indian tribes that passed along the same road gave Berlandier valuable information for his Indian studies; a major reason for being a member of the Boundary Commission. He studied them intimately.

["On the days we were there indigenes of different nations came to gather around the hut of which I have spoken, There was a Bidai, some Kickapoos, a Cherokee, a Tejas, a Chickasaw, and a family of Caddos. All spoke completely different languages but when together they could understand one another most perfectly by means of signs.

"The Bidai was an old chief, poor, dirty, clothed in a bad bison skin; his belly was covered with a dry rash and his footgear was in accord with his other garments. His nose was compressed and convex up above.

"The Tejas was also an old man of some fifty or sixty years, and obviously well known in Nacogdoches where he was known by name as Indio Bautista. He had come with some Creoles who esteemed him highly because of his honesty. That man was badly scarred from Smallpox; his height was five feet six at least, and he was dressed in leather. On one of his arms he wore four iron bracelets and on the other a single bracelet of brass.

"The Caddo was established with his wife under a sort of awning close to us and where he lived in a bed practically the entire day and intentionally exposed to the smoke of a fire that was kept burning to repel insects. The man had a silver plaque suspended by means of a ring of the same metal from the membrane between his nostrils and on the plaque was engraved a cross. That same kind of ornament among his people sometimes extends to their chins and those who wear it are obliged to set it aside to eat and drink.

"Of all, the Kickapoos were quite well dressed after the fashion of poor Scottish Highlanders. Their heads were decorated with plumes, or with a sort of toque [a woman's small brimless hat] garnished with silver plaques. Like all savages, they had a taste for painting their faces but if lacking preferred vermillion they make use of ground charcoal that gives them a terrifying aspect.

"The only Cherokee that passed there was noticeably a drunkard. I noted on him some rudiments of hieroglyphic paintings and roughly drawn to seem as a sort of map of the courses possibly of some rivers in Texas. His warlike and bellicose tribe numbering close to two thousand, print today a gazette written in their mother tongue accompanied by a translation into English.

"Their aspect is quite similar to that of the Americans, and like them they are proud and arrogant. A handkerchief on his head simulated a turban; their belts and the rest of their dress give them the aspect of some Muslims. Moving in from the east of the United States of America they every day encroach farther and farther on the soil of Texas and at the same time ceding their eastern lands to the United States. They trespass more and more on Mexican soil where they are still only partly settled and where a large number of them later established themselves with the permission granted to them by General Terán. [Likely to win their friendship and allegiance in case of a Texas Revolution, though that never happened] (Paraphrased from Volume IV Chapter 3)]

While camped there, some Anglos passing by warned the members of the Commission that some Chicas that had followed them ever since the Trinity were believed with the intention of stealing their horses and mules [the Anglos] somewhere along the way. One especially known for his wrongdoings had been near them for the past day or so that, when warned about, the Commission had suspicion of him and distrust.

Justly or unjustly having taken him for a spy, it was made known to him that with any wrongdoing he would be held responsible and that all punishment would fall on him and him alone. Frightened by the threat, he and his companions likely changed their views and did not cause any trouble. Moreover, the dragoons were well armed as were all other members of the Commission.

Some several days later beyond the Brazos and when on the Colorado, some soldiers were sent to hunt bison accompanied by the Kickapoo Indians. During the hunt they perceived in the distance some Tawakonis who were Comanche allies signaling to them as if being friendly. But being outnumbered by them and believing that their pretence of friendless was really treacherous, the party returned without responding to the beckons.

That same day the two dragoons that had been sent to Béxar for medications and other provisions, and had just returned, apprised the Commission it was known in Béxar that just recently the same band of Tawakonis had killed a man near Béxar which increased the pains taken with respect to the security of the Commission's camp that day located not far from where the Tawakonis had been seen.

On June 15, two days after leaving the Colorado, the Commission reached the San Marcos River known to arise not far from the western branches of the Brazos but losing its name when reaching the Guadalupe. Berlandier wrote of the San Marcos:

["Among the many tree species one can find there I shall cite the nut trees [pecans] as being very common, as well as a species of cherry which is esteemed in the countryside. In the environs the soldiers called to my attention a small, pretty shrub known as palo dulce [also known as vara dulce, *Eysenhardtia texana*].

"June 16-18. From the San Marcos to Béxar the distance is eighteen leagues from the San Marcos to the Guadalupe; seven leagues from the Guadalupe to the Arroyo del Cibolo [Stream of the Bison], and five leagues from there to the capitol of Texas [then San Antonio]. The aspect of the countryside all along the way is most agreeable broken by occasional streams, hills, plains, and forests where lovely vegetations prevail." (Paraphrased from Volume IV Chapter 3)]

["On the eighteenth of June after a journey of sixty-six days over an immense wilderness and a thousand privations, we [Berlandier, Chowell, Batres and dragoon escorts] finally arrived at the point of our departure without having been able to reach our desired destination. However, thanks to the recommendations of General Terán for us to return safely and to improve our health, and to the kindness of the inhabitants of Béxar we again made a long and agreeable sojourn there." (From Volume III Chapter 3 of *Journey to Mexico*)].

Notes: The following is paraphrased from John C. Ewers, Editor of Berlandier's *The Indians of Texas in 1830.*

["On June 18 the party reached San Antonio 66 days after leaving that town on their difficult trips eastward as far as the Trinity. Berlandier recovered his health, made a round trip later that summer to Matamoros by way of Laredo (Route "D" on the **Frontispiece**) and was back in San Antonio in the early fall when in November and December he spent one month with the Comanche Indians on a bison and bear hunt."]

Chapter Twelve
THE BISON AND BEAR HUNT

It was in November of 1828 two years after Jean Louis Berlandier had arrived in Tampico, Mexico, in December of 1826 that the French/Swiss naturalist had his first real encounters with the usually hostile though at rare times peaceful Comanche tribes and profited by learning of their knowledge and medicinal uses of native plants.

To early-day students of Texas ethnology as was Berlandier, the native peoples were generally thought of as "untamed Savages with ancient ways of life and customs," often barbaric and unworthy of any rightful consideration for the "Brotherhood of Civilized Man." Among the many tribes in Texas the Comanches (**Fig. 4** warriors) were considered to be the most cunning of them of treachery, silent stealth and death to anyone not one of their own or closely allied.

["Ranked as the most expert of warriors, the Comanche at night is the most dangerous of them when crawling into camps and bivouacs to steal horses. He will in his efforts harmlessly pass near to a sleeping man when with one thrust of his knife or blow of a tomahawk might silence him forever but woe-betide to the man who discovers him and attempts to interfere with his favorite pastime, that of stealing horses." (Col. William Irving Dodge, *Our Wild Indians: Thirty-three Years' Personal Experience*)]

Of similar thinking Berlandier penned:

["The Comanches constitute the largest, most powerful, and most feared tribe of them all anywhere in the territory of the Mexican Republic. They are riders of consummate skill but equally capable of long marches on foot and to go on a raid wherever he likes, and that like is to make war on enemies but also the hunt. They are equally capable with the bow, gun, and the lance.

"Moreover, the murder of someone not of their own people is so indifferent to them that they have no moral compulsion against it, and as such a deed will also earn one a feather and raise his status among his peers.

"By the terrors of their unholy raids and murders, Comanches spread great fear among Texan settlers and Mexican villagers on both sides of the Rio Bravo." (Berlandier's *The Indians of Texas in 1830*)]

While in Mexico City awaiting departure of the Boundary Commission Survey of Texas, Berlandier spent time visiting some of the old ruins of the ancient Toltecs and numerous villages still lived in by "pure indigenes" that spoke the "Azteque tongue and were totally ignorant of the Spanish language or anything of Christianity." They were, however, "quite hardworking."

Berlandier learned of the pyramids of Teotihuacán and of beautifully erected and ornately carved stone monuments that "inspired elevated opinions" of ancient Americans. Berlandier saw and learned of "antiquities esteemed as quite remarkable in the history of human civilization." (Berlandier, Volume II Chapter 3).

Yet, only a few months later Berlandier began venturing into the areas of nomadic peoples of the north who knew little of anything akin to civilization, or construction of anything more than crude huts of tree branches or thatch, and/or teepees made of animal hides. Soon, he learned of and observed, first hand, of the "indolence, ignorance and laziness" among aboriginal nomads to the north in Mexico quite different from Middle Americans in the far south who in their past had built pyramids, temples, plazas and monuments, and had knowledge of writing, calendars, mathematics and astronomy.

As quoted of the general nature of the indolent aborigines to the north, and in particular the Carrizos south along the Rio Grande and west of Matamoros, Berlandier wrote in his *The Indians of Texas in 1830*, paraphrased:

["The Indian nomads are ill-clad and dirty. They suffer greatly from hunger and they often go naked. They may make do with deer hides for clothing although women may also wear old worn-out cloth dresses given to them in the villages, but the people in general are utterly disgusting in appearance. All of them paint their faces and sometimes their whole bodies with vermillion and a complete absence of eyelashes and eyebrows are considered necessary among them."]

The Carrizos that Berlandier encountered spoke of Comanche raids deep into Mexico south of the River and when the peaceful Carrizos moved close to haciendas for some measures of protection. There were a few Carrizos in and around Laredo for the same reason and occasionally Lipan Apaches who camped nearby to the presidio also in fear of hostile Comanches.

During his 1828 travels to the eastern regions of Texas, Berlandier learned of Comanche raids and those of their allies, the Tawakonis, on Texan settlers as in Chapter Nine of this book, and attacked by them often (Bond). Bollaert wrote of travels in Texas through the same areas of Berlandier in this novel: "We travel with a good lookout for a person is never safe in the Indian ranges" and accordingly Berlandier and his companions traveled with an escort of thirty dragoons well armed with rifles and lances.

It was early in March of 1828 when in Béxar that Berlandier first saw a few, friendly, Comanches in and around the villa where they traded and bartered deer and buffalo hides for settler calicos and trinkets as well as pots and pans. But not until November of that year when again in Béxar that Berlandier had an opportunity to associate closely with Comanches in peace and that happened when at the invitation of Chiefs Reyuna and El Ronca, Berlandier and Colonel Ruiz joined them on a bison and bear hunt.

It occurred deep into the truly wilderness areas of Texas west of Béxar not yet inhabited by anyone other than an Indian. Those areas were for a century already, Comanche territory and where few other tribes dared to venture except when at war.

Berlandier jumped at the opportunity to venture into Comanche lands because it would give him an opportunity to observe and collect natural history and geological specimens up on the higher elevations of the region [later to become known popularly as the Texas Hill Country]. Furthermore, he would have opportunity to learn, first hand, much about the Comanche people [later to become a major portion of his book on the Indians of Texas].

At the time, Colonel Ruiz was in command of the Béxar presidio Alamo de Parras and took with them an escort of thirty dragoons for protection in case of need, not so much against any turncoat Comanches but against any of the other Indians as the Lipan Apaches who might attack their arch Comanche enemies while en route, Such would likely involve the Ruiz party and that fear did raise two alarms of attacks during the hunt.

The following account of the bison and bear hunt is excerpted and paraphrased at length from Berlandier's own words in Volume IV Chap. 4 *Journal to Mexico during the Years 1826 to 1834*.)

It is now November-December, 1828.

* * * *

For a long time now we had been desirous of exploring the western parts of Texas but because of the insecure peace with the savages—a peace which was often interrupted by sudden hostilities—we did not dare visit those very interesting and little-known regions. Although it had been about a year since the Comanches had signed a tentative peace with General Bustamente, few had yet come to Béxar to trade in the markets.

But in August of 1828 Chief Barbakista, the most celebrated and most valiant of the great Comanches, came to renew the bonds of amity with the people of Texas and principally in the environs of Béxar. Celebrated in the annals of Comanche warriors he was received with good wishes as the moderations in his demands had helped to inspire confidence in him and he was showered with gifts.

Moreover as it so happened in November of 1828, some fifty to eighty Comanches led by a chief named Reyuna came to the presidio. Following the suggestions of Col. Ruiz, though apprehensive, we decided to go out into the wilds with them and participate in a mutual hunt. It would give me much opportunity to know more about them and of their aboriginal customs.

On Wednesday morning of November 19, 1828, our party left Béxar and we made only about three leagues [one league being about three miles] the first day towards the northwest, and where we camped on the edges of a stream called Arroyo de los Olmos [Stream of the Elms]. Mingling with a confusion of nomadic men known for savagery and treachery and still somewhat fearful of them, I believed of myself to have been transported to those remote eras in which primitive men lived in the wilds and still in the infancy of a future civilization.

The eighty some Comanches with us of warriors, wives and children had more than three hundred horses among them in their caravan equal to about eight per every man, woman, and child. To the Comanche, tribal wealth is in the numbers of their horses. Our progress that first day was imposing because of all the people and the many animals and surprisingly of the silence which prevailed in the wilderness and among our savage travel companions.

We spread out over a great distance travelling in single files or en masse, while a certain number forming an advance guard went ahead to spy out the land. Even the Comanches have warring enemies but at the Arroyo de los Olmos we had already begun to observe a great difference in the character of the Comanches who accompanied us. In the towns and villages they are more suspicious, more taciturn, and more mysterious, and never do they manifest that gay and open nature which they have when out alone in the wilds.

["In the presence of strangers the Indian is reserved and silent but in the wild nothing could be further from truth. Away from strangers, the Indian is a noisy, jolly, rollicking, and mischief-making jokester." (From Dodge. *33 Years among Our Wild Indians*)]

After the women and children set up their camp, having erected the conical tents which are made of skins, they also spread hides and prepared spots for the repose of their absolute masters who either lie down or go hunting leaving all the labors of the camp to the women. Towards evening the men gathered in a place away from the camp to smoke a pipe.

["The women are slaves to the men who do not work but who occupy themselves only with war and hunting. The women bring in the animals that are killed and cut and cure the meat, then tan the hides, make clothes for the men, and care for the horses." (Sánchez, *A Trip to Texas in 1828*)]

["If a Comanche man should ever do any work such as getting water or wood, or setting up tents, he would be ridiculed by all the rest of the tribe." (Bianca Babb, *A True Story of my Life and Capture by the Comanche Indians*)]

["Only the women worked. In Comanche estimation, a man degrades himself by doing anything that had the appearance of manual labor which is why they could not be enticed into the missions where work was expected of the men. I once saw an Indian man riding on a horse and carrying nothing while his wife afoot was bent over with a heavy load on her back.

"The husband owns the wife entirely. He may abuse and beat her, even kill her without question, or even be sold or given away or offered to another man for sexual pleasures without her consent. In fact, it can be considered an affront if by the offer that a guest in the tent refuses the use of her even by his unmarried brothers but when they are married reciprocity is expected.

"Their hard life and constant work tell upon them very soon and by the time that a woman is sixteen years of age, and likely having been married as young as ten or twelve, and likely having been impregnated soon after the onset of menses, very little of her youthful freshness is left. Indeed, it is almost impossible after about the age of sixteen to make from appearances even an approximate guess at the age of any Indian woman. I know a married woman of eighteen who looks as old as her mother who must be thirty-five and already herself old looking, and this is not at all unusual." (Paraphrased from Dodge, *Thirty-three Years Among Our Wild Indians*)]

Among the Indians who came with us there were two men prisoners who labored as slaves believed to be Mexicans taken from their families in their youth. Although they are recognizable as to their origin there is something particular to be noted about them—the same as their masters—the absence of eyelashes, eyebrows, and a beard which had been plucked out. This disfigures them in an extraordinary fashion and gives them an aspect difficult to describe.

On November 20 we awoke early half-pierced by the cold and left the Arroyo de los Olmos en route to the Arroyo del León (Stream of the Lion), the headwaters of the Medina River, and then to the Ojo de Agua (Eye of Water) where we camped. It was in the environs of that camp that an indigene killed a deer and shared it liberally among all.

The continual state of war in which these Indians live puts them on the guard and subjects them to irrational fears. It was for such a reason that after a tranquil day without having any trace of an enemy, that two false alarms burst among us. Besides the fact that the Comanches had behaved with good faith towards us, even in forming a single camp with them, that prudence obliged us to gather to ourselves in one spot around which we placed our armed dragoons.

["War has always been the pleasure and passion of the Indian. They live for war and with or without cause, tribes occupying lands adjacent to each other were almost constantly on the warpath." (Dodge, *33 years Among Our Wild Indians*)]

From the tents closest to the arroyo came the cries of *Tasi, Tasi* [Lipans, Lipans] and the sounds of uneasy horses around us made us think that it was indeed an attack by the Lipans—enemies of the Comanches—and of which we had already been cautioned. We all took up our arms but nothing was comparable to the activity of the warriors who rushed towards the place from where the cries had come and in less than one or two minutes everyone was ready for combat. We even observed some of the women with bows in hand ready to defend themselves while others gathered their children in close around our tents, undoubtedly believing to be the safest place for protection with the dragoons there. What had caused the horses to be alarmed was eventually thought to have been a foraging bear or a prowling jaguar not uncommon to the region.

One day early in our trek we camped on a small hill where we could keep watch on all our horses and not far from there a stream of limped water flowed in the midst of a charming plain. The Indians and the soldiers killed some deer and a few bears there but two Comanches who had gone much farther than the others succeeded in killing two bison of which they brought back some pieces of meat but left the rest for carnivorous scavengers.

Scarcely had the sun gone down a few degrees below the horizon when another alarm of Lipans spread among the Comanches, but persuaded by the frivolity of their fear we scarcely paid any attention to them. The warriors however mounted and again spent the evening making patrols without discovering anything. Yet, fears of attacks by any enemy forces always kept them vigil of enemy signs as well as those of us who could get caught up into a conflict between warring tribes.

Very early the next morning without any new alarms of hostile indigenes we started off for the banks of the Guadalupe where we arrived towards the middle of the day and on the western bank where we camped and encountered some hunters from Béxar who had killed a large quantity of bear. We camped on a spot suitable for bear hunting from the many signs of them although we did not see one. On the other hand that afternoon we saw many bison out in the environs but waited until the following day to hunt them. We went out in the morning in the company of Colonel Ruiz and not far we found some, probably while drowsing and unaware of our stealth. Colonel Ruiz killed a small bison but the dragoons too soon went after it and the others fled.

I believe at this point it would not be remiss to write a few words about the hunting of bison; that mammal which furnishes an abundant subsistence to the Indian tribes in these parts. The hunting of them is performed in different ways and at different seasons according to the uses which is proposed to make of bison. The savages that make that animal their chief meat provender hunt it at any time. In the summer, bison are devoid of any thick hair and their hides are good for little. Towards the end of autumn and at the beginning of winter, principally in November and December, the bison have thicker hair and herds of them advance as far south as the environs of Béxar. Before such a large number of them had been killed they crossed the banks of the Rio Grande, and the chronicles of bygone days tell us that they visited Nuevo León south of the river at that period. Most of the inhabitants of Texas profit from that migration towards the south, but everywhere the military and civilians hunt both bison and bear with the former for meat and the latter for lard. Both animals supply good pelts.

When hunters encounter bison in herds on the plains, they can attack them in two ways. In the first method, a good marksman dismounts and while hidden behind an intelligent horse trained for that kind of hunting he approaches the animals. Without bridle or saddle the horse knows to slowly advance towards the bison while also cropping the grass up to within range of the firearm. The bison accustomed to seeing wild horses in such action do not take fright.

During that time other hunters mounted on very fast horses have silently posted themselves in the defiles to kill the bison on the run when they try to flee. If he who had dismantled has the good luck to kill a single animal, and if his companions have not been seen, they as a team are masters of many in the herd.

At the sound of the first shot, bison will go off in a gallop but the wounded one soon drops and the rest may stop and surround him to the scent of his blood and low plaintively. It is then that the skillful hunter profiting from that circumstance can kill them all on the spot if as may happen they gather around the wounded, particularly if the hunter is well hidden. I have known hunters who have killed as many as twenty in that manner in only a half-hour.

But still another chase less punishing and less dangerous can be done in all areas, particularly in the forests by the stealth of an approaching hunter hiding behind trees and shrubbery.

Yet in any situation, a wounded bison of several hundred pounds in weight is apt to charge that is not good for the hunter if he has already spent all of his arrows or with only a single-shot firearm for any measure of defense.

The second method consists in chasing them on swift horses with a bow in hand. The indigenes have a great advantage in that method as their powerful bows can sometimes send an arrow all the way through a bison. They can race alongside at the speed of one (**Fig. 5**) and shoot as many arrows at them as they please.

When their quivers are exhausted they retrace their steps to find the wounded and dying and those animals already dead. That chase is often dangerous but only practicable on the plains or in certain valleys or anywhere if a hunter has been sighted and the bison are already on the run.

On December 3, we left in the morning following differing courses to eventually reach the headwaters of the Guadalupe towards which the tracks of all the wild animals were directed and during the day we saw not too far away three large herds of bison. They crowned the hills which seemed to be moving. Their heavy but swift pace; their dorsal humps; the hair of their heads and the tuffs on their knees; and their entire appearance in mass gave them a terrifying air.

On December 4, we spent three days in the same camp from which the hunters carried out their hunts in every direction. On one of the excursions which we made with Colonel Ruiz in the forests of cypress [likely to have been junipers] where we first saw and first wounded a large black bear. We followed it for a long time on horseback though not until the end of a quarter of an hour that it finally succumbed.

In the afternoon of December 8, we abandoned camp and set out towards the gorges that we could see in the distance of the most agreeable mountains in Texas [the Hill Country] known as the *Cañon de don Juan de Ugalde* [Uvalde]. The forests [motes] of oaks were all about and of other trees already devoid of leaves for the winter season. The next morning a dense fog covered the surface of the earth scarcely allowing us to recognize the direction in which we needed to get to the canyon still some distance away. As we travelled thus, unable to distinguish objects even if only of a short distance, some male bison that we suddenly saw allowed us to approach very closely without yet their having perceived us.

Colonel Ruiz posted himself behind a tree and shot at one of the bison but being only wounded it ran off impossible to follow because of the fog. When one thus shoots one of these animals at too close a range it is necessary to take refuge behind a tree as did Ruiz, for if a bison is only wounded and has seen the fire, and if so enraged, it may charge the spot where it believes to have discovered its adversary.

We found the *Cañon de don Juan de Ugalde* to be one of the prettiest sites in Texas and five to six leagues in length. As it widens, one can see immense prairies covered with verdure where the deer graze on grass alternating with large oak forests roamed by bears feeding upon acorns. On the edges of the valley and especially on those of the principal stream [Frio River] one finds a unique kind of nut tree [believed to be the walnut] with very small fruit similar to a large hazelnut and with an extremely hard shell. But much of the nearly one week that we stayed in the environs of the canyon and in the uplands, the frequent rains largely kept us confined to our tents.

On the 14th we left the canyon and spent the night in a small valley known as the Arroyo Seco [Dry Stream] but on occasions it evidently flowed with water. Its banks like those of the Frio are frequented by wild horses whose tracks are seen everywhere but despite their abundance we were not able to see a single one of them no matter what searches we made for them during the day's travel.

But in looking for them we were struck with admiration at how well country life can accustom a man's eyesight to distinguish the presence of alien objects at a distance in the wilds, but still more to recognize from the least sign the traces of most of the animals. The indigenes surprised us every occasion to where we had not seen anything, they called our attention to the hoof prints of a wild horse, and we observed the differences which exist between the latter and that of one of our mounted horses, and whether the pace was fast or slow. A skilled Indian hunter can also distinguish the tracks of bison from those of wild cattle, and I have been surprised to see Indians follow the tracks of a deer over rocky terrain where no imprint could be easily seen.

On December 15 we split up into two bands because lacking fresh meat we still wanted to go in search of wild cattle. But without finding them we then travelled in search of the other soldiers who had agreed to camp on the opposite bank of the Arroyo Hondo [Deep Stream].

On December 16 we departed from the Arroyo Hondo skirting its banks for a long time. Its bed was dry for the entire travel but we found it covered with sycamores and nut trees [possibly pecans in the bottoms but walnuts up on tops]. Everywhere however could be seen proofs that the stream like the Seco could swell like a torrent and then roll along enormous blocks of limestone having fallen from neighboring cliffs into the stream courses. The names of the Arroyos Seco and Hondo are names suited to their names of being both deep and dry.

On December 17 we struck camp at sunrise and crossed small hills covered with mesquites. Wild horses were common there foraging on them, as well as the two species of deer known as *venado* [deer] and *berrendo* [pronghorn]. The former like the bison form herds of one sex and the males are the ones that congregate the least. In November and

December when they begin to rut they seek companions; the time when they are most easily hunted.

After another five leagues of travel we arrived at the banks of the Medina River where within were catfish and in the environs turkeys roosting at night up into the trees. Bobcats seize the prey that a hunter kills from a tree and scarcely does a turkey fall that if the hunter does not seize it on the spot the ferocious carnivore may disappear with it into the underbrush.

December 18. From the western banks of the Medina we reached Ciudad de Béxar after a day's travel of close to ten leagues, almost directly from the west to the east with an inclination of some degrees from south to north. The closer that we drew to the city the more that we recognized the obvious traces of immense inundations from recent floods, likely from the heavy rains that we had experienced days before in the *Cañon de don Juan de Ugalde*, though obviously heavier. The San Antonio River had left its usual banks and had threatened houses generally badly constructed or made of earth, and brought on sad memories of the year 1817 when a flood cost the lives of many victims.

Finally after thirty days of travel in the midst of the wildest wilds of Texas without seeing a single hut of civilized man we entered the city well after dark. Our friends there had been uneasy about us because a false rumor had been spread around that when at the headwaters of the Guadalupe the Indians betrayed us and had stolen our horses to leave us afoot for the long trip back.

Such hadn't happened to the relief of everyone but instead we had, through the whole time of the hunt, learned much of the more amiable sides of the Comanches when we had camped together with little problems and when on two occasions that we feared attacks by Lipans, we stood prepared to battle them together.

* * * *

In conclusion to his diary account of the thirty days spent with the Comanches in the "Wilderness where no white men lived" Berlandier wrote:

["Before ending this Chapter I should make some mention of what we have just experienced, that these vast regions of wild Texas are so little known. Some of the maps that we used have a great deal to be desired with what is relative to Texas. The most exact of them is owed to the colonization of Texas and principally to the entrepreneur Mr. Stephen Austin who has gathered much information on the locations of rivers and landmarks and distributions of the indigenes, and most recently published.

"On some of the maps there are a number of nomadic nations unknown to me by the names used. But along with my assignment to collect plants and animals for my Geneva sponsors, I also had the responsibility to report on the Indians of Texas north of the Rio Bravo del Norte to the Mexican Ministry of the Interior. The observations are largely mine, although mixed with the information provided by others of my contemporaries and those who I met along the way."]

Notes: Berlandier's sources were mainly those of General Terán and Lieutenant Sánchez on the tribes of east Texas; General Bustamente on the Lipan Apaches; and Colonel Ruiz on the Comanches and their close allies, the Tawakonis. Berlandier no doubt learned more of the same and/or of other Indians from talking with the pioneer Anglo settlers who he encountered during his many months of travels. There was too, no doubt, the military in the presidios where he visited whose responsibilities were to protect the citizens of Mexico from Indian raids.

Other people wherever encountered and who had suffered from Indian depredations no doubt spoke freely and graphically of experiences, often those of burned cabins, deaths to members of families and/or abductions of young girls and women of child-bearing ages. Furthermore, there were the losses of crops, stolen horses and cattle, all as discussed in Chapter Nine, *Encounter with the Foleys*. Good but disturbing-to-read references are *Indian Depredations in Texas* by pioneer J. W. Wilbarger; *Louisa of Woods' Crossing, A Story of the Texas Frontier* by James Kaye; and *A Fate Worse Than Death; Indian Captives in the West, 1830-1885*, by Gregory and Susan Michno.

A BRIEF SUMMARY OF
BERLANDIER'S LIFE AND
ACCOMPLISHMENTS

In 1826, Jean Louis (Jon Louie) Berlandier (1805-1851) was born in rural Fort de l'Écluse near the French border with Switzerland and where in neighboring Geneva he trained as a botanist and a pharmacist. In his early twenties, in 1826, Berlandier sailed on the American built schooner, the *Hannah Elizabeth*, to Tampico, Mexico, and from there on horseback to Mexico City.

It was there that he joined the Mexican Boundary Commission as a biologist and plant specialist for a scientific expedition into the little known areas of Texas north of the Rio Bravo del Norte The Commission left Mexico City on November 10, 1827, under the command of Brigadier General Manuel de Mier y Terán, arriving at Laredo on February 2, 1828, and during the ensuing months of March, April, and to the end of May, Berlandier made plant collections in the area of Laredo and then northerly between San Antonio, Gonzales, and as far beyond San Felipe as the west banks of the Trinity River [**Frontispiece** Route "A"]

By the time of his arrival on the Trinity, Berlandier was quite ill from malaria and enough so to have to return to Béxar for recovery [**Frontispiece** Route "B"]. While there and when able, he collected other plants and animals and made notes on the indigenous Indians of the region.

Much of his studies on the Comanches, a major portion of his later book, occurred in the months of November and December, 1828, while back in Béxar and accompanied Colonel José Francisco Ruiz along with an escort of 30 Mexican dragoons on a bear and bison hunt in the wilderness areas northwest of San Antonio [**Frontispiece** Route "C"]. The hunt was at the invitation of Comanche Chief Reyuna who was then friendly to Mexicans and to Anglo-Americans in the San Antonio area.

While deep in Comanche territory in the San Saba River area, Ruiz and Berlandier investigated a "silver mine" area reportedly near to the site of a long ago abandoned San Saba Spanish Presidio. There had been since the 1700s, reports of silver mines in the region and said to be rich in pure silver and gold that had been used by the Indians to make jewelry. Such belief persisted in myth and lore and even appeared on old maps and a 1820s map of Texas made by Stephen F. Austin and used by Berlandier and Ruiz. Nothing of importance however, seems to have been found along the San Saba since Berlandier makes no mention of any mines in his diary.

> ["At the presidio of San Saba abandoned for more than sixty years there is nothing left but the bulwarks where the Indians sometimes go to lodge. They call the ruins Casas Viejas and if the cordon of Mexican presidios is ever extended westward it would be an important point to occupy. The San Saba River flows close to the old fortification providing water there without having to go far for it. The Comanches with us call the river *Tsoko-ka'ani-humo.*" (Paraphrased, and being the last entry at the end of Volume IV Chapter 4)]

Route "C" in the **Frontispiece** is that of the bison and bear hunt in November and December, 1828 that essentially ended the two year Boundary Commission exploration of Texas.

Route "D" concerns a five week journey during July and August of 1828 to Matamoros through Laredo and back again to San Antonio for the purposes of satisfying prearranged agreements to rejoin General Terán and Lt. Sánchez in Matamoros after their return from a two month planned exploration of the Nacogdoches and San Augustine areas.

It was while there and much of their purpose that Terán and Sánchez gained much information about the eastern Indian tribes supplied to Berlandier for his *The Indians of Texas in 1830.*

Berlandier then settled in Matamoros, Mexico, seemingly a favorite place of his where he became a physician in a local hospital as well as a pharmacist in the community providing service especially to the sick and needy. Moreover, while there, Berlandier married a Mexican girl and had several children with her although little is known of them; not even of their names. It is reasonable to assume that Berlandier met her during his 1828 trip to Matamoros, and be reason enough for him to settle there.

He then was only twenty-three years of age and she likely an alluring young teen-aged *señorita* as most were at that young age. It was and is still a custom among Latin American peoples for young girls to celebrate their coming of age as *quinceaneras*, or fifteen year-olds and be considered marriageable.

Moreover, records of plant materials sent to Geneva by Berlandier show that some were shipped from Matamoros in November of 1830 and July of 1831, not long after his being in Matamoros in July of 1828. It can be assumed that he met his future wife sometime during those years when she was, likely, a teenager and he a young man in his twenties.

Such would be the only hint of a romance in Berlandier's life and briefly touched on by Lt. Darius N. Couch U.S. Army who wrote in an 1854 letter after Couch had purchased Berlandier's extensive botanical and animal collections from his "widow" for the Smithsonian and other Institutions. Couch wrote of him and how learned of him (paraphrased):

["Berlandier followed a custom common in Mexico and that was for a man to live with a woman as his mistress but not marry her until later."]

The result of this connection was likely one of several years as several children were born to them and one of them reportedly to being a Captain of Mexican Infantry.

Until his death by accidental drowning in December of 1851 at the young age of 46, Berlandier continued to collect plant and animal specimens in numerous areas of southern Texas up to the lower Colorado region, and areas around Cópano and Aransas Bays. He further collected in the Kingsville area and from there along a route to Goliad where he made extensive collections, as well as in northeastern Mexico south of Matamoros.

His further investigations were important to both biology and ethnology but they were largely the results of his own initiative in observing and collecting both specimens and data in the field and in conversations with knowledgable men not members of the Boundary Commission.

One such man was Dr. Samuel George Morton, a Philadelphia physical anthropologist interested in interracial marriages and their progeny, and who was seeking information on crossbreeding in the lower animals. The last known of Berlandier's contributions to science was the information sent to Dr. Morton in 1851, the year Berlandier died, on the hybridization of wolves, coyotes, and dogs in Mexico. The data is on file in the Gray Herbarium Library at Harvard University (John C. Ewers, Editor, Berlandier's *The Indians of Texas in 1830.)*

In all, Berlandier's collections of many hundreds of plants are located in twenty-seven world herbaria, and many hundreds of insects, mollusks, reptiles and birds, as well as mammals, manuscripts, maps, journals, and drawings, and collections of historically important Indian artifacts mostly of the Comanche Indians, and all that are housed in several prestigious Institutions as the Smithsonian Institution, United States National Museum, Gilchrest Museum, Library of Congress, and in the Libraries of Harvard, Yale, Texas A&M University, College Station, and The University of Texas, Austin. The original diary handwritten in French is housed in the U.S. Library of Congress.

Berlandier's voluminous diary of some 1,500 pages of travels and adventures is the basis of this novel: *Berlandier; A French Naturalist on the Texas Frontier.*

* * * *

"Berlandier is remembered as one of the most enlightened naturalists and ethnographers of the American West during the frontier period." *John C. Ewers*, Ethnologist

"Among Berlandier's manuscripts, none is of greater value than his *Voyage au Mexique par Louis Berlandier pendant les années 1826 à 1834*, handwritten in French and preserved in the Library of Congress." In his introduction to Berlandier's diary published in English and entitled simply as *Journal to Mexico*, Muller (1980) believed that Berlandier "ranks high among plant collectors, and not only did he discover much of interest to botanists, he inspired the efforts of field men for a century." *C.H. Muller*, Botanist

"In the history of Texas botany, Berlandier will be remembered as the first of the profession to have investigated the flora of the Gulf Coastal Plain, the Balcones Escarpment and the Edwards Plateau, all famous collecting grounds for plants, and that his name will be remembered in the genus *Berlandiera* [and by the Texas Green-Eyed Sunflower (**Back Cover**)]." *Susan Delano McKelvey*, Botanist

"Berlandier lives on posthumously in the many scientific names of organisms named in his honor including such as the Texas Windflower, *Anemone berlandieri* (**Plate 1**); The Rio Grande Leopard Frog, *Rana berlandieri* (**Plate 3**); and the little gnome-like Texas Tortoise, *Gopherus berlandieri* (**Plate 4**)." *Edward O. Moll*, Biologist

Epilogue

IN DEFENSE OF JEAN LOUIS BERLANDIER

Samuel Wood Geiser wrote that "Mankind must have its heroes but also its scapegoats and scientific men are no exceptions." Geiser felt it wrongful that Jean Louis Berlandier could be considered a "scapegoat" in exploration and collection of plants in Texas and Mexico. But years later in his memoirs, Augustin Pyramus De Candolle, the famous Swiss author of the *Prodromus* of the botany of the world, accused Berlandier of being "a malcontent and an ingrate."

De Candolle complained of "dried plants in small numbers, badly chosen and badly prepared, and that Berlandier had neglected completely the sending of animals and seeds and the communication of notes on the country." De Candolle further complained that at the end of some time, Berlandier "neglected even to write, so that for a long period it was not known if he was alive or dead." It was then found that while "some sixteen thousand francs had been spent for dried plants the number received were not worth a quarter of that amount."

But Dr. John Briquet, De Candolle's successor in the directorship of the Botanical Garden at Geneva, commented quite to the contrary in Berlandier's defense. Briquet was of the opinion that botanical explorations in Texas and Mexico were carried on at times under difficult field conditions, depredations, and dangers hard to believe in Europe to "citified" biologists. And despite De Candolle's criticisms it should be remembered, in truth, that Berlandier collected many thousands of specimens including plants and animals in which there were a great number of new species. Briquet stated it "rash to believe" that Berlandier's worthy accomplishments were "made in vain to the little coterie of botanists at Geneva."

More to be said in reference to Briquet's comment of "a time under difficult conditions," and further to Berlandier's defense a few facts can be added to this treatise to understand the conditions under which Berlandier had worked, offering some qualification of the harsh judgments that have been passed over on determination of his achievements.

With lucid eloquence, early explorers described the difficulties and dangers of collecting in Texas; the swift north winter winds effecting drops of thirty degrees of temperature in as many minutes; the summer heat and high humidity; the torrential rains which seemed at times as if the heavens had opened; the torments of droves of gadflies and gnats by day, and incredible swarms of pesky mosquitoes by night. Sánchez y Tapia who traveled with Berlandier wrote of the "thick swarms of mosquitoes" that bothered them considerably. "May the Lord have pity on us," all bewailed. Sánchez further wrote, paraphrased:

["On May 10 after leaving San Felipe and finding a place to stop for the night, Berlandier and I lay up on the cargo with some hope for the slightest of breezes, but to the unbearable heat were added the continuous croaking of frogs though the night, and legions of mosquitoes that bit us everywhere and kept us from sleeping a wink. When the longed-for dawn broke we saw a terrible onslaught that the cursed insects had made upon us, leaving us full of swollen spots, and especially on the face of the General which was so raw that it seemed as if it had been flayed." (José María Sánchez y Tapia, *A Trip to Texas in 1828*)]

In his further defense of Berlandier, Geiser questions in what ways that these kinds of hardships of which there were many for weeks on time, and attested to by Berlandier, Terán, and Sánchez, may have affected Berlandier's responsibility for the "nonperformance" of his duties, if *that* could be construed the fact to the dissatisfaction of his Genevese patrons. Geiser believed that the answers were worthy of several considerations. First and foremost, collections faithfully made were ruined by conditions of weather for which Berlandier could hardly have been held responsible.

Of one storm and heavy rain in particular, Sánchez wrote (paraphrased):

["At about five one afternoon the sky was covered by thick clouds and it seemed as if all the winds blew furiously at the same time. By about six a most terrible storm was raging and the rain was so heavy that it seemed the entire sky, converted to rain, was falling on our heads. The woods were afire with the vivid flashes of lightening, and nothing but a continuous rumbling of thunder was heard. The shock of the shrill howling winds was horrible and the storm continued until eight o'clock that next morning. I gave thanks to the Almighty that we survived such a furious storm."]

An account of another storm is written:

["At Gonzales, at about two o'clock on the morning of April 18, 1828, the expedition encountered a furious thunder and rain storm when just the afternoon before, Berlandier had spent several hours in extensive collections of plants. The storm was a tropical thunderstorm lasting until four o'clock, followed by a light rain that did not cease until eight o'clock. Berlandier's plants were wet through necessitating the shifting of them into new driers taking the next two hours. Tents were no protection to us against such deluges; even in the General's tent protection was to be had only by covering himself and his bed with buffalo robes. Subsequently, the weather was hot and humid; proper drying was impossible; and the mildewing of plants was an unavoidable consequence."]

Again, when General Terán's train was halted by a broken wheel west of the Colorado [April 22], and Berlandier had time to collect intensively, his efforts were brought to naught by heavy rains that fell during a considerable part of the late afternoon. Thus, such conditions logically explain the "poor" preservation of any of Berlandier's plant specimens complained of by De Candolle as being "badly prepared."

But a second consideration of importance to difficulties was that specimens may, actually, have departed in reasonably good condition but arrived less so when for weeks at a time on long voyages specimens were stowed in the damp holds of sailing vessels with poor to no ventilation; water always in the bilges; and the humidity always high. Even sails made of canvas and ropes made of hemp turned moldy in damp lockers and likewise crackers and like foods, and crew's cotton clothing and linen bedding being always damp. Books and maps and anything made of paper were subject to mold and mildew, especially the old newspapers in which the plants were pressed.

In addition, the difficulties of transportation to seacoast ports for shipments of specimens were an obstacle that materially reduced the ease and/or the effectiveness of Berlandier's efforts. Sánchez wrote of the difficulty of travel on muddy roads during May, 1828:

["We continued our march where the ground was so full of water, and there were so many mud-holes, it was necessary for the soldiers and the drivers to pull out vehicles and even the mules at times by hand. For this reason we were barely able to travel much more than four leagues (one league equaling about three miles) during the entire morning and part of the afternoon.

"The road continued through country with low marshes and such serious mud-holes that it was necessary to pull out the vehicles and mules and the soldier's horses by hand almost at every step because they sank so deep in the mud. With terrible fatigue we traveled about three leagues, and then the axle on one of the baggage wagons broke and we were obliged to halt. But then a furious rain came down that lasted until midnight, after which it continued to drizzle all the rest of the night, the ground being turned into a lake and where and when we were in the most pitiable condition imaginable.

"Along the way there occurred a great mud-hole, and in order to cross it, it was necessary to unload the baggage and to take it across on mules, a task that lasted until midday. As we were crossing a small creek, the shaft of the instrument wagon was broken and it became imperative to remain on the spot."]

Of like difficulties during the Texas Revolution, the Mexicans wrote of heavy pieces of artillery "bogging down to the axles on muddy roads at every turn of the wheels." In slogging along over muddy lands considered as quagmires, José Enrique de la Peña wrote of "sinking up to my knees in mud, falling, and getting up and finally taking off my boots and continuing thus."

Despite such hardships Berlandier collected many thousands of plants and of such animals as insects, mollusks, birds, mammals, and reptiles, and most were accounted for during long stays in Laredo, San Antonio, Goliad, and Matamoros. His specimens today are found in twenty-seven world herbaria (seventeen in Europe and ten in the United States) including some of the most prestigious as the Kew Gardens in England; other herbaria in Paris, Madrid, Berlin, Copenhagen, and Vienna for examples; and as well in the Gray Herbarium, Harvard, and Smithsonian Institution, Washington D.C..

From April 25, 1827 and November 15, 1830—in just three and a half years—Berlandier itemized 188 packets of dried plants totaling some 55,077 specimens; 198 packets of plant seeds; 935 insects; 72 birds; 55 jars and bottles of material in alcohol; and more than seven hundred specimens of land and freshwater mollusks, amounting to more than 1,350 specimens collected per month on average during the three and a half years, or about 50 per day.

It may be thought for some reason(s) that De Candolle didn't receive all of the items shipped (lost along the way?). However, Berlandier's manifest lists 2320 "numbers" sent of which records in Geneva actually show 2351 received (or thirty-one *more* than Berlandier reported); all of the evidence needed that the shipments claimed by Berlandier reached their destination. Therefore, De Candolle had little basis for his erroneous and grossly ill-conceived in-appropriate claim of Berlandier having "neglecting completely" the shipping of them.

If it seems odd that Berlandier apparently made no effort to defend himself against De Candolle's criticisms then there may be underlying reasons never to be known that may also explain why he never returned to France. But, at least, De Candolle must have felt *some* need to name a new genus in Berlandier's honor, *Berlandiera,* in the Asteracea (Aster or Sunflower Family), and to name *B. texana* (Texas Green-Eyed Sunflower, **Back Cover**) as the designated type species.

And as one example, for where and when such species as the above were described, the type species *Berlandieri texana* appeared in De Candolle's own monumental seventeen volume *Prodromus* (the flora of the world) in Vol. 5:517, dated 1836, just ten years after Berlandier went into Texas to collect plants and after De Candolle had already become critical of his work.

There are other sunflowers named by Augustin Pyramus De Candolle in Berlandier's honor, such as *Gynoxys berlandieri* and *Senecio berlandieri* that may have been some additional measures of De Candolle's later remorse for his criticisms and ways to rectify them. Moreover, in later years Alphonse De Candolle (a son) admitted that "it was not improbable that some of Berlandier's pressed specimens were badly distributed, overlooked, and lost." But it may, too, have been that Berlandier himself felt a failure to not send more plants to De Candolle due to the adversities and difficulties experienced in the collections as those described above and attested to by Lt. Sánchez.

Berlandier alone knew what cost him his health and enthusiasm in the rigors of harsh weather, periods of extreme sickness, and difficulties of travel including always the fears and threats of hostile Indians. Berlandier was fatigued by the monotony of living in a semi-savage state of life and tired of the ignorance and superstition of the indigenous peoples, even including the "rabble" of the lower *mestivo* classes. Nevertheless, a young man only in his early twenties amassed a remarkable number and variety of specimens—many new to science—to which he dutifully felt obligated to do and admirably done to accomplish the objectives of his assignment to the *Comisión*.

In his treatise of the Texas Tortoise (**Plate 4**) Edward O. Moll summed up Berlandier's accomplishments as follows: "By the time of his death [1851], he had vindicated himself and regained the honor that had been taken from him by the De Candolle debacle. He had become affluent in his adopted homeland but more importantly he had become loved and respected."

In 1853, two years after Berlandier died, Lt. Darius. N. Couch U.S.A., who bought the naturalist's collections from his widow for the

Smithsonian Institution, wrote that Berlandier was "universally beloved for his kind, amiable manners, and regard for the sick poor of the city, being always ready to give advice, care, and medicine to such without pay."

As a last matter in this defense of Berlandier's plant collections (those sold after his death), it is important to say that the quality of them, reflective to all of those collected in Berlandier's era, were quite acceptable in condition. In a letter, Harvard botanist Asa Gray wrote that the Berlandier collection was a "great mass of good working specimens as good as Drummond's Texas collections."

In another letter Gray wrote (paraphrased): "Let me say that the Berlandier collection will be quite important and as useful to me as I ever supposed it would…there is a vast deal in it which I am exceedingly glad to have."

In his Introduction to the publication of Berlandier's diary, *Journey to Mexico*, Dr. C. H. Muller believed that Berlandier "still has lost little of his botanical significance" and "to all of what is already known of the man there still remains a rich and untouched area." Muller concluded that "to those who would delve more deeply into the life of the man a rewarding can be guaranteed for the effort."

Such a "rewarding" occurred to this author while researching the literature for this book written in the popular form of a historical novel. It also happened in compiling Appendix "A" to list at least sixty species and subspecies named in honor of Berlandier's many contributions to natural science, along with including photographs of a few of the major biota (**Plates 1-5**).

Any Texas student majoring in biology will always remember the Texas Green-Eyed Sunflower, *Berlandiera texana* (**Back Cover**); the Rio Grande Leopard Frog, *Rana berlandieri* (**Plate 3**); and especially the little-in-size but well-known Texas Tortoise, *Gopherus berlandieri* (**Plate 4**) sometimes seen with a red face after feeding upon the ripened fruits of prickly pear cactus.

BIBLIOGRAPHY

Allen. Thomas B.
  1974.   *Vanishing Wildlife of North America*. Nat'l
          Geographic Soc., Wash. D.C., 208pp.

Babb, Bianca
  1926.   "A True Story of my Capture by, and Life with the
          Comanche Indians." Unpub. MS. The Texas State
          Historical Assoc. (?) The Univ. of Texas, Austin.

Baker, James K.
  2010.   "Berlandier; A French Naturalist on the Texas
          Frontier." Jour, of South Texas, Fall 2010. Vol. 23,
          No. 2, pp42-53.

Berlandier, Jean Louis
  1826.   M*emoire Sur La Famille des Grossulariees*. Memoires
          De La Societe De Physique Et D'Histoire Naturelle
          De Geneve (3:43-69)

  1846.   *Itinerariio: Campaña de Palo Alto y Resaca de
          Guerrero*. Yale University Western American
          Collection MS S-310.

  1847(?) *Journal of Jean Louis Berlandier during 1846-1847*
          (Including the time when he was driven from
          Matamoros by the Americans). Thomas Phillips
          Collection, MS 15512 (Berlandier), Library of
          Congress, Washington D.C. Copy at the Amulfo L.
          Oliveira Library, University of Texas at Brownsville.

  1969.   *The Indians of Texas in 1830*. John C. Ewers (Ed.).
          Translated by Patricia R. Leclercq. Smithsonian
          Institution Press, Washington. 209pp. (The original
          Manuscript of some 330 pages written in French
          was entitled *Indigene nomades des Etats Internes
          d'Orient et d'Occident des territories du Nouveau
          Mexique et des deux Californies*, dated 1830. Ewers

shortened the work to its present title in English.)

    1980.   *Journey to Mexico during the Years 1826 to 1834.* Two Volumes translated by Shiela M. Ohlendorf, Josette M. Bigelow and Mary M. Standifer. The Texas State Historical Assoc., Univ. of Texas at Austin. 672pp.

Berlandier, Louis [Jean Louis], and Rafael Chovel

    1850.   *Diario de vaiage de la Comisión de Límites que puso el Gobierno de la república, bajo la dirección del exmo. Sr. general de division de Manuel de Mier y Terán, Mexico City: Tipographía de Juan R. Navarro, 1850.*

Boethel, Paul C.

    1959a.   *History of Lavaca County.* Revised Edition. Von Boeckmann-Jones, Austin, Tex.172pp.

    1959b.   *Sand In Your Craw.* Von Boeckmann-Jones, Austin, Tex. 134pp.

    1967.   *On The Headwaters of the Lavaca and the Navidad.* Von Boeckmann-Jones, Austin, Tex. 192pp.

Bollaert, William

    1850.   "Observations on the Indian Tribes in Texas." London Ethnological Society Journal, Vol. 2. London.

    1956.   *William Bollaert's Texas.* Univ. of Okla. Press, Norman. 421pp.

Bond, Mary C.

    1988.   "Book mentions prominent pioneer." Seguin, Tex. Newspaper. "Family Tree," May, page 4.

Brice, Donaly E.

    1987.   *The Great Comanche Raid.* Eaken Press, Austin, 122pp.

Brown, John Henry

    1978.   *Indian Wars and Pioneers of Texas.* Reprint of 1880 ed. By Southern Historical Press, Easley, SC. 1152pp.

Cantrell, Gregg

    1999.   *Stephen F. Austin, Empresario of Texas.* Yale Univ. Press. New Haven. 493pp.

Catlin, George
> 1995. *Letters and Notes on the North American Indians.* Two
> Volumes in One. JG Press. 291pp.

Clopper, Joseph Chambers
> 1828. "J.C. Clopper's Journal and Book of Memoranda
> for 1828." *Quarterly of the Texas State Historical
> Association* XIII (July 1909): 44-80.

Couch, Lt. Darius N. U.S.A
> 1854. Letter to Spencer Fullerton Baird. Quoted in
> William Healey Dall, *Spencer Fullerton Baird; A
> Biography.* (Phila. 1915), 322,

De la Peña, Lt. Col. José Enrique
> 1975. *With Santa Anna in Texas; A Personal Narrative of
> The Revolution.* Translated By Carmen Perry. Tex.
> A&M Univ. Press. College Station. 202pp.

Dodge, Colonel Richard Irving
> 1884. *Our Wild Indians: Thirty-three Year' Personal
> Experience among the Red Men of the Great West.*
> Archer House, NY. 657pp.

Ewers, John C.
> 1970. "John Louis Berlandier: A French Scientist
> among the Wild Comanches of Texas in1828," in
> *Travelers on the Western Frontier.* Ed. John Francis
> McDermontt, Urbana, Ill.
> 1997. *Plains Indian History and Culture; Essays on Continuity
> and Change.* Univ. of Okla. Press, Norman. 272pp.

Fehrenbach, T.R.
> 1974. *Comanches, The Destruction of a People.* Alfred A.
> Knoph, NY. 537pp.

Gatschet, Albert
> 1891. The Karankawa Indians. *Archaeological and
> Ethnological Papers of The Peabody Museum*, vol. 1,
> No. 2. Harvard University, Cambridge, Mass.

Geiser, Samuel Wood
> 1948. *Naturalists of the Frontier.* Dallas So. Methodist
> Univ. Press, 296pp.

Gray, Asa

    1854 (?) *Herbarium Berlandierianum Texano-* Mexicanum Archives, Gray Herbarium, Harvard University, Cambridge.

Humfreville, Jacob Lee

    2002. *Twenty Years Among Our Hostile Indians.* Stackpole Books, Mechanicsburg, PA. Jackson, Jack (ed.) and John Wheat (translator). 480pp.

    2000. *Texas by Terán; The Diary Kept by General Manuel de Mier y Terán on His 1828 Inspection of Texas.* Univ. of Texas Press, Austin. 300pp.

Jenkins, John Holmes III (Ed.)

    1995. *Recollections of Early Texas.* Univ. of Texas Press, Austin. 307pp.

Johnston, J. M.

    1924. "A Neglected Paper by Jean Louis Berlandier." *Contributions from the Gray Herbarium of Harvard University*, new series LXX 87-90.

Jones, C. Allen

    2005. *Texas Roots*; Tex. A&M Press, College Station. 256pp.

Kaye, James

    2007. *Louisa of Woods' Crossing.* Xlibris Corp. 353pp Including a comprehensive Treatise on the pioneer history of Texas settler and Indian conflicts.

Kelly, Fanny

    1990. *Narrative of my Captivity Among the Sioux Indians.* Chicago: Lakeside Press. R.R. Donnelley & Sons, Co. (Edited by Clark and Mary Lee Spence) 367pp.

Le Jeune, Paul

    1634. *Relations des Jésuites de la Nouvelle- France de 1634.*

McKelvey, Susan Delano

    1956. *Botanical Exploration of the Trans- Mississippi West, 1790-1850.* Arnold Arboretum of Harvard University. 1144pp.

Michno, Gregory and Susan

    2007. *A Fate Worse Than Death; Indian Captives in the*

West, 1830-1885. Caxton Press, Caldwell, Idaho. 527pp.

Mills, Betty J.
    1985.   *Calico Chronicle*. Texas Tech Press, Lubbock.191pp.

Moehring, Sharon Anne Dobyns
    2004.   *The Gonzales Connection: The History and Genealogy of the DeWitt and Jones*. Trafford Publishing, Victoria, Canada. 416pp. Chapter 2-15.

Moll. Edward O.
    2003.   *Gopherus berlandieri (Agassiz, 1857) - Texas Tortoise*. Tucson Herpsociety

Neighbors, Robert S.
    1852.   "The Na-u-ni, or Comanches of Texas," in Henry R. Schoolcraft, *Historical and Statistical Information Respecting the History, Condition, and Prospects of the Indian Tribes of the United States*, Vol. 2, Philadelphia.

Padilla, Juan Antonio
    1919.   "Texas in 1820: Report on the Barbarous Indians of the Province of Texas." Translated by Mattie Austin Hatcher. *Southwestern Historical Quarterly* XXIII (July, 1919): 46-68.

Pinkava, Donald J.
    1967.   "Biosystematic Study of Berlandiera (Compositae)." Brittonia: Vol. 19, No. 3 (Jul-Sep., 1967), pp. 285-298.

Ruiz, José Francisco
    1972.   *Report on the Indian Tribes of Texas in 1828*. Edited by Georgette Dorn, New Haven. Yale University Library, 1972.

Sánchez y Tapia, José María
    1828.   *Archivo General de Guerra y Marina, Fracción 1, Legajo núm. 7, Mexico City.*
    1926.   "A Trip to Texas in 1828." Translated by Carlos E. Castañeda. *Southwestern Historical Quarterly*, XXIX (April 1926): 249-288.

Smithwick, Noah
  1958. *The Evolution of a State or Recollections of Old Texas
      Days*. Compiled by Nanna Smithwick; Donaldson,
      Austin. Univ. of Texas Press. 307pp.

Terán, General Manuel de Mier y
  2000. *Texas by Terán*. Ed. Jack Jackson, translated by John
      Wheat. Univ. of Texas Press, 300pp.

Willbarger, J.W.
  1889. *Indian Depredations in Texas*. Hutchings Printing
      House, Austin. 691pp.

Appendix A

BERLANDIER TAXONOMIC NOMENCLATURES

Botanical:

Agavaceae
> *Dasylirion berlandieri* S. Watson (Blue Sotol, Zaragosa Blue Twister)

Amaranthaceae
> *Sarratia berlandieri Moquin* (Fringed Amaranth)

Apocynaceae
> *Macrosiphonia berlandieri* A. Gray (Flor de San Juan)

Arecaceae
> *Brahea berlandieri* Bartlett (Rock or Sombrero Palm)

Asteracea: (Asters, Daisies, or Sunflowers)
> *Berlandiera* A.P. de Candolle
>> *B. lyrata* G. Bentham var. *lyrata* (Green Eyes, Lyre Leaf Green Eyes)
>> *B. monocephala* (B.L. Turner) Pinkava
>> *B. pumila* (A. Michaux) T. Nuttal (Soft Green-eyes.) Sy=*B. tomentosa* (Pursh) Nuttal
>> *B. subacaulis* (Nuttall) Nuttall (Florida Green-eyes)
>> *B. texana* A.P. de Candolle, 1836, (Texas Green-eyes, or Texas Green-Eyed Sunflower **Back Cover**)
>> *B. texana x betonicifolia* (W. Hooker) J.K. Small
>> *B. texana x macrophylla* (A Gray) M.E Jones
>> *B. texana x humilis* J.K. Small
> *Cacalia berlandieri de Candolle*
> *Eupatorium berlandieri de Candolle*
> *Gnaphalium berlandieri de Candolle*
> *Gutierrezia berlandieri* A. Gray

Gynoxys berlandieri de Candolle var. *cordifolia*
Pectis berlandieri de Candolle (Berlandier Chinch Weed)
Perymenium berlandieri de Candolle
Pseupogynoxys berlandieri (de Candolle) Cabrera
Senecio confuses syn. *S. berlandieri* (de Candolle) Hemsley (Mexican Flame Vine)
Stevia berlandieri A. Gray (Sweet Leaf or Candy Leaf)

Boraginaceae
Ehretia anacua (Terán & Berlandier) I. Johnston "Sandpaper Tree"

Brassicaceae
Lesquerella berlandieri A Gray

Cactaceae
Echinocereus berlandieri (Engelmann) Haage (Berlandier's Hedgehog Cactus)

Campanulaceae: (Bluebells)
Lobelia berlandieri A. Gray (Berlandier's Lobelia) var.*brachypodia* (Gray) McVaugh

Chenopodiaceae
Atriplex berlandieri Moquin (Salt Bush)
Chenopodium berlandieri Moquin (Berlandier Pitseed Goosefoot)
Obione berlandieri Moquin, de Candolle

Euphorbiaceae
Croton berlandieri Torrey (Pepperbush)
Jatropha berlandieri Torrey (Baseball Plant)

Fabaceae (Leguminosae)
Acacia berlandieri Benth. (Guajillo)
Astragalus crassicarpus Nutt. var. *berlandieri* Barnaby (Groundplum)
Mimosa berlandieri A. Gray ex Torrey (Berlandier's Mimosa)
Mimosa pigra L. var. *berlandieri* (A. Gray) B. Turner (Giant Sensitive Plant)
Sophora segundiflora (syn *Calia erthrosperma* Terán and Berlandier) Texas Mountain Laurel

Juglandaceae

Juglans microcarpa (Berlandier & R. Chovell) "Texas Black Walnut"

Linaceae: (Flaxes)

Linum berlandieri W. Hooker var. *berlandieri* (Berlandier's Flax)

Sy= *Cathartolinum berlandieri* (W. Hooker) J.K. Small

Sy= *L. rigidum* F. Pursh var. *berlandieri* (W. Hooker) J. Torrey & A. Gray

Sy= *L. berlandieri* W. Hooker var. *filifolium* L. Shinners

Malvaceae

Abutilon berlandieri A. Gray ex S. Watson (Berlandier's Indian Mallow)

Nyctaginaceae

Acleisanthes berlandieri A. Gray "Berlandier's Trumpets"

Acleisanthes obtusa (Berlandier) "Four O'clock"

Oleaceae

Fraxinus berlandieriana de Candolle (Berlandier or Mexican Ash)

Onagraceae: (Primroses)

Calylophus berlandieri E. Spach (Texas Primrose or Berlandier's Sundrops)

Calylophus berlandieri E. Spach subsp. *berlandieri* (E.Spach) H. Towner & P. Raven

Calylophus berlandieri E. Spach subsp. *pinifolius* (G. Engelmann ex A. Gray) H. Towner (Square-bud Primrose)

Oenotheria (Hartmannia) berlandieri Nutt. (Mexican Evening Primrose)

Oxalidaceae

Oxalis berlandieri Torr. (Shrubby Oxalis)

Poaceae

Phragmites australis (Cav.) Steud. subsp. *berlandieri*

Phragmites berlandieri E. Fournier. (Carrizo, Giant Reed)

Ranunculaceae

Anemone berlandieri Pritzel (Texas Anemone or Ten Petal Thimbleweed; **Plate 1**)

Rutaceae
> *Esenbeckia berlandieri* Baill (Berlandier's Jopoy)

Solanaceae
> *Lycium berlandieri* Dunal. (Berlandier's Wolfberry)

Verbenaceae
> *Citharexylum berlandieri* B.L. Robbins (Berlandier Fiddlewood)
> *Lippia berlandieri* Schauer (Mexican Oregano)

Vitaceae
> *Vitis berlandieri* Planch var. *tomentosa* Planch (Winter Grape)
> *Vitis berlandieri* Planch *x vinifera* Linnaeus (Common Grape)
> *Vitis berlandieri* Planch *x riparia* Michaud (Frost Grape)
> *Vitis berlandieri* Planch *x rupestris* Scheele (Riverside Grape)

Molluscan:

Polygyridae: (Scrubsnails)
> *Praticolella (Helix) berlandieriana* (Moricand 1833),
> Berlandier's Practicolelle; Banded Snail or Scrub Snail;
> **(Plate 2)**

Unionaceae
> *Lampsilia berlandieri* Lea (Pearl-bearing Mussel)

Amphibian:

Ranidae
> *Rana (Lithobates) berlandieri* Baird (Rio Grande Leopard Frog;
> **Plate 3**)
> > Sy= *R. halecina [pipiens] berlandieri* (Coues & Yarrow)
> > Sy= *R. pipiens berlandieri* Schmidt

Reptilian:

Testudinidae
> *Gopherus berlandieri* (Agassiz) Stejneger (Texas Tortoise **Plate 4**)
> > Sy= *Xerobates berlandieri* Agassiz

Avian:

Troglodytidae
> *Thryothorus [Troglodytes] ludovician berlandieri* Baird
> (Berlandier's Wren)

Mammalian:

Cricetidae: (New World Rodents) *Sigmodon hispidus berlandieri*
(Berlandier Cotton Rat; **Plate 5**)

Mustelidae

Taxidea taxus berlandieri Baird (American Badger)

Soricidae

Cryptotis parva berlandieri Baird (Least or Short Tailed Shrew)

Appendix B

THE INDIAN TRIBES OF TEXAS

(Based upon Jean Louis Berlandier, José María Sánchez, Juan Padilla, José Francisco Ruiz, Manuel de Mier y Terán, and Stephen F. Austin)

Adai - Addaîze - Aguajes - Aînais - Alabama Coushatta - Anadarko - Apache - Aranama - Arapaho - Ay - Belocsis - Bidaises - Biloxi - Caddo - Caihuas - Carancahueses - Carrizo - Chariticas - Cherokee - Cheyenne - Chicas - Choctaw - Coahuiltecan - Cocos - Comanche - Conchates - Cujanos - Delaware - Eyeish - Hainai - Iguanees - Jumanos - Kichai - Kickapoo - Kiowa Apache - Kiowa - Koasati - Kohani - Lipan Apache - Mapas - Mescalero Apache - Nabedache - Nacasils - Narcissi - Nacogdoches - Nadacos - Navadoches - Ocosaus - Orcoquisacs - Osages- Pacanabos - Pawnee - Quapaw - San Pedros - Shawnee - Sonsores - Tahuacanos - Tamaulipas - Tawakoni - Tawehash - Tejas - Temayacas - Tenichites - Tonkawa - Waco - Wichita - Yamparicas - Yowane - Yucanticas.

Spellings of the above tribal names vary in the literature differently among the English, French and Spanish explorers, as well as by the pioneer colonists of other nationalities and languages. Examples of differing spellings are "Wacos" also known as "Huecos" and "Karankawas" aka "Carancahueses" or "Tarancahueses." Moreover, the tribes had their own names common to them in their own languages. For example, Tonkawas called themselves *Tickan-wa-tics*. The Lipans called their own people *Tindi* while the Comanches called Lipans *Tasi*. The Tonkawas aka Tancahueses, or spelled as Tancahues, are known as *Yani* to the Lipans or *Caricoë* to the Comanches. The early-day French explorers and fur traders called the Tonkawas *Konkones,* but the Kiowas called them

Ku-ikogo or *Kadiko*. The pioneer settlers often just called them *Tonks* as Americans are sometimes just called *Yanks*.

Among the Indians, themselves, were derogatory slang names for enemies. The Tonkawas called Comanches "Snakes" and sign language for them was an index finger wiggling backwards across the chest signifying a snake crawling along. The French Black Robes in the northeast called the Woodland Indians *Sauvages*; the Spanish Brown Robes in the southwest called the Plains Indians *Barbaros*; and for like reasons of well known barbarity the early day Dutch traders of the eastern seaboard called them *Barbaars*.

The names given to some tribes or sub-tribes by early Spanish and French explorers into Texas are difficult to equate with more recent tribal names, and by Berlandier's time the great majority of the Texas tribes had already lost their identities when becoming but small remnants of once larger tribes. Berlandier made a determined effort to identify, locate, and estimate the populations of those Indians still living in East Texas and on the Gulf Coast in 1828-1830, as well as those on the Plains of the same era. "Small remnants" of tribes in Berlandier's time were as few as only a small number of members of closely related families that still exist.

For examples, Berlandier wrote of the Ocosaus as being only 80 to 100 individuals in 20 to 25 families living along the Rio Neches and the Trinidad River. Also on the Trinidad there were only 20 to 30 families of the Chicas. Of the Nadacos on the Sabine, only about 150 individuals of 30 families remained.

Other tribes of Berlandier's interests were those from east of the Mississippi who sought refuge from expanding white settlements prior to 1828. But in three decades from the time of Berlandier in the 1820s through the 1830s-1840's Texas Revolution, Mexican War, and Texas Statehood, and by the 1850s growth of civilization and "civilization vices," nearly all of the Indians of Texas of which Berlandier wrote were either virtually exterminated or driven out of the State. By 1840, Bollaert knew of only three remaining Tejas Indians but extinct by 1843 and also by then the Jumanos, the Cocos, the Karankawas, and the Coahuiltecans had disappeared completely and/or had been absorbed into other, related, tribes and subsequently lost to their original identity.

Furthermore, French explorers in Texas as De La Salle and Henri Joutel, the diarist who kept journals of their expeditions in the 1500s, wrote of more than 51 tribes in Texas still unknown to modern-day ethnologists.

It is believed by Ewers (1969) for all of the above in Berlandier's research, that Berlandier must have had access to a number of French and Spanish diaries and other early-day historical papers on the Spanish period of Texas. Moreover, it is known that Berlandier drew heavily from the knowledge of his contemporaries and travel companions as Manuel de Mier y Terán, José Francisco Ruiz, José Sánchez, Juan Padilla, and Stephen F. Austin, as well as the many of the pioneer settlers of Texas from whom Berlandier gained first-hand accounts.

Note: It needs to be stressed at the end of this novel that while aboriginal peoples of the frontier era were generally thought to be "unworthy of the Brotherhood of Man," such belief largely ceased by the end of the 1800s and early into the 1900s when the two cultures of Native Americans and those of European origins began to intermix and become one people.

Appendix C

THE *HANNAH ELIZABETH*

Little is known of the schooner *Hannah Elizabeth* on which Berlandier sailed to Mexico in 1826 although his Diary in Vol. 1, Chapter 1 describes her as an American vessel. Nothing more is said of her as to where and when built and/or of what length, tonnage, or how rigged. But by definition and in fact, a schooner-rigged vessel has at least two masts and as many as three or more rigged with fore-and-aft sails. Some also have square topsails. The main mast in its aft position was (is) taller than the foremast as depicted in **Figure 1.**

The gaff-rigged schooners common of the times as the one pictured were used for fishing the Grand Banks off Newfoundland but also carried cargos and passengers throughout the Great Lakes and up and down the east coast of the United States and into the Bahamas. They also sailed to ports in the Gulf of Mexico and down to those in the West Indies and in South America as well as across the Atlantic to Europe.

There were two other sailing vessels of Berlandier's time also named *Hannah Elizabeth* and his diary gives 12/24/1826 as the date of arrival aboard the (his) *Hannah Elizabeth* in Tampico, Mexico. In harbor records that date ship arrivals in Tampico a *Hannah Elizabeth* (the same?) arrived in Tampico, Mexico, on 3/19/1827 and that was captained by Charles Roding. There is also a record of the (a) *Hannah Elizabeth* arriving in Tampico, Mexico, on 9/14/1827 and captained by Charles Riling (Roding?). While the two vessels may have been the same schooner they were apparently sailed by different captains not unusual on different voyages or even to fly different flags.

The three-month difference between the 12/1826 and 3/1827 dates of arrival in Tampico suggest that sometime after Berlandier arrived in the (his?) *Hannah Elizabeth*, the same schooner took a shorter voyage to other places; perhaps to Havana, Cuba, New Orleans, Louisiana, or

Kingston, Jamaica and back again to Tampico. The six month difference between arrival dates in Tampico of 3/1827 to 9/1827 suggests time enough for the same schooner to have sailed back to Le Havre de Grâce, France, and then return to Tampico.

There is a report of an American schooner also named *Hannah Elizabeth* arriving in Nassau, The Bahamas, on 7/5/1834. It was likely the 67' schooner of that same name known to have been built in Stoningham, Connecticut, in 1829 and that sailed through western Atlantic waters including the Bahamas to then, later, when in the Gulf of Mexico, run aground and sink at the Pass Cavallo entrance to Matagorda Bay, Texas, on November 19, 1836. However, since the schooner of the Pass Cavallo sinking wasn't built until 1829 it could not have been the same *Hannah Elizabeth* that sailed from France to Mexico in 1826.

In still another instance of identical names, a brig-rigged *Hannah Elizabeth* with square sails was reported in Tampico, Mexico, in January, 1830. A related account, likely of the same brig is that in June, 1835, Colonel James Fannin bought 152 West African slaves in Cuba and sailed them to the Brazos River Brazoria area of Texas aboard the "slave ship" *Hannah Elizabeth*. The number of slaves aboard suggests the "slave ship" was the above mentioned Brig that may also have been in Tampico.

Appendix D

ILLUSTRATIONS

Front Cover: *Along the Rio Bravo Del Norte*, Charles Marion Russell ca 1913.

Back Cover: Texas Green-Eyed Sunflower, Ber*landiera texana* A.P. de Candolle; Photograph by Jeff McMillian.

Frontispiece: Routes of Berlandier's Travels in Texas in 1828. Based upon the 1829 map of Stephen F. Austin and that of the National Museum of Natural History.

Figure 1: *Hannah Elizabeth,* after a painting by Georgina Nemethy; "Schooner at Sea."

Figure 2: Route of the schooner *Hannah Elizabeth* from France to Mexico.

Figure 3: Gonzales to San Felipe road crossing of Lavaca River; Photograph by Cathy L. Baker.

Figure 4: Comanche Warriors; Archives of The University of Texas, Austin. ca1860.

Figure 5: *The Buffalo Hunt* by Charles Marion Russell ca.1894.

Plate 1: Texas Windflower (*Anemone berlandieri*); Photograph by John R. Gwaltney, Southeasternflora.com.

Plate 2: Berlandier Banded Scrub Snail (*Practocolella berlandieriana*); Photograph by Tim Ross.

Plate 3: Rio Grande Leopard Frog (*Rana berlandieri*); Photograph by Gary Nafis.

Plate 4: Texas Tortoise (*Gopherus berlandieri*); Photograph by Jason Penney.

Plate 5: Berlandier Cotton Rat (*Sigmodon hispidus berlandieri*); Photograph by James Gathny, U.S. Center of Disease Control.

Appendix E

ACKNOWLEDGMENTS

Appreciation goes to Cathy L. Baker for the Figure 3 photograph taken of where the Old Gonzales to San Felipe Road crossed the Lavaca River and where in April of 1828 that Jean Louis Berlandier and the Mexican Boundary Commission camped for a night.

Further appreciation for information on Jean Louis Berlandier goes to Mary Markey and Deborah Stultz of the Smithsonian Institution; Ann Kaupp of the U.S. National Museum of Natural History; the Arnulfo L. Oliveria Library at The University of Texas, Brownsville; The University of Texas Archives Library, Austin; and the Texas State Historical Association.

Chapter Nine information on the Washington Green Lee Foley and John Samuel Woods families is from biographer Willie F. Woods, III.

Picture permissions and credits go to Georgina Nemethy for the Figure I painting of *Schooner at Sea;* plant and animal photographs in Plates 1-5 and Back Cover are attributed to John R. Gwaltney, Tim Ross, Gary Nafis, Jason Penney, James Gathany and Jeff McMillian.

Appendix F

ABOUT THE AUTHOR

James Kaye is a retired biologist from the National Park Service first at Carlsbad Caverns, then Padre Island, Joshua Tree, Death Valley, Channel Islands, and lastly Hawaii Volcanoes National Park where he researched problems of non-native plants and animals competing with endemic species and ecosystems. After retirement Kaye sailed his 36' gaff-rigged ketch on a twenty-seven day 3,000 mile voyage to Washington State where he lived for several years and sailed up into Canadian waters and down the Pacific Coast to San Francisco.

Kaye now lives in his home State of Texas and has written a novel based on the pioneer history of the area, that of a true person and a real location entitled *Louisa of Woods' Crossing; A Story of the Texas Frontier* and that in large part is relative to subjects in this book. Additionally relevant, there is an article by Kaye on the life of Berlandier published in a history journal, and another history journal subject concerning events in the 1836 War of Texas Independence.

Other interests are in the works of Victorian era painters with two articles published in art journals on English artist John William Waterhouse co-authored with Cathy L. Baker and a novel by Kaye based on the artist and one of his true life models.

Over many years Kaye published widely in a variety of science journals on plant and animal subjects as well as being a long distance sailor, scuba diver, and a sailplane and single engine airplane pilot. Kaye is now mostly a writer with this book being his most recent work combining interests in biology and history.

Plate 1: Texas Anemone, Windflower, or Thimbleweed
(*Anemone berlandieri*)
Photograph by John R. Gwaltney

Plate 2: Berlandier Banded Scrub Snail
(*Practicolella berlandieriana*)
(Line = 10mm) Photograph by Tim Ross

Plate 3: Rio Grande Leopard Frog
(*Rana berlandieri*)
Photograph by Gary Nafis

Plate 4: Texas Tortoise
(*Gopherus berlandieri*)
Photograph by Jason Penney

Plate 5: Berlandier Cotton Rat
(Sigmodon hispidus berlandieri)
Photograph by James Gathany